Being a Reader™

Funding for Center for the Collaborative Classroom has been generously provided by:

The Annenberg Foundation

The Atlantic Philanthropies (USA) Inc.

William and Allison Bennington

Booth Ferris Foundation

The Robert Bowne Foundation, Inc.

The Annie E. Casey Foundation

Center for Substance Abuse Prevention,
    U.S. Department of Health and Human Services

The Danforth Foundation

The DuBarry Foundation

Einhorn Family Charitable Trust

The Ford Foundation

Google Inc.

William T. Grant Foundation

Evelyn and Walter Haas, Jr. Fund

Walter and Elise Haas Fund

The Horace Hagedorn Foundation

J. David & Pamela Hakman Family Foundation

Hasbro Children's Foundation

The Charles Hayden Foundation

The William Randolph Hearst Foundations

Clarence E. Heller Charitable Foundation

The William and Flora Hewlett Foundation

The James Irvine Foundation

The Jenesis Group

Robert Wood Johnson Foundation

Walter S. Johnson Foundation

Ewing Marion Kauffman Foundation

W.K. Kellogg Foundation

John S. and James L. Knight Foundation

Lilly Endowment, Inc.

Longview Foundation

Louis R. Lurie Foundation

John D. and Catherine T. MacArthur Foundation

A.L. Mailman Family Foundation, Inc.

MassMutual Foundation

The MBK Foundation

Mr. & Mrs. Sanford N. McDonnell

Mendelson Family Fund

MetLife Foundation

Charles Stewart Mott Foundation

William & Linda Musser

National Institute on Drug Abuse,
    National Institutes of Health

National Science Foundation

New York Life Foundation

The New York Institute for Special Education

Nippon Life Insurance Foundation

NoVo Foundation

Karen and Christopher Payne Foundation

The Pew Charitable Trusts

The Pinkerton Foundation

The Rockefeller Foundation

Louise and Claude Rosenberg, Jr. Family Foundation

The San Francisco Foundation

Shinnyo-en Foundation

Silver Giving Foundation

The Spencer Foundation

Spunk Fund, Inc.

Stephen Bechtel Fund

W. Clement & Jessie V. Stone Foundation

Stuart Foundation

The Stupski Family Foundation

The Sulzberger Foundation, Inc.

Surdna Foundation, Inc.

John Templeton Foundation

U.S. Department of Education

The Wallace Foundation

Wells Fargo Bank

Small-group Teacher's Manual

CCC Collaborative Literacy

Being a Reader™

SET
3

Center for the
Collaborative
Classroom™

First edition published 2016.

Being a Reader and CCC ClassView are trademarks of Center for the Collaborative Classroom.

Front cover illustration by Jing Jing Tsong, copyright © Center for the Collaborative Classroom

Illustrations by Michael Wertz, copyright © Center for the Collaborative Classroom

Center for the Collaborative Classroom
1001 Marina Village Parkway, Suite 110
Alameda, CA 94501
(800) 666-7270; fax: (510) 464-3670
collaborativeclassroom.org

ISBN 978-1-61003-816-4

Printed in the United States of America

2 3 4 5 6 7 8 9 10 RRD 24 23 22 21 20 19 18 17

CONTENTS

(continues)

CONTENTS *(continued)*

Lessons

Appendices

Introduction

Overview of Small-group Reading

The Small-group Reading strand of the *Being a Reader*™ program provides targeted, differentiated reading instruction that is appropriate for readers at their individual reading levels. Students are grouped with others at a similar stage of development and then matched with texts at the appropriate level. The small-group instruction is organized around high-quality, carefully selected texts in a variety of genres that are assembled into 12 leveled sets. As the sets progress, they increase in sophistication and complexity.

The *Being a Reader* Program

The *Being a Reader* program is a yearlong curriculum for grades K–2 in whole-class and small-group instructional settings. The program has been carefully designed to nurture students academically and socially while providing rigorous instruction in early literacy skills and strategies. *Being a Reader* lessons also provide specific instruction to develop students' ability to work independently and take responsibility for their learning and behavior. The strong foundation in independent work makes it possible for you to work with small groups of students to provide differentiated instruction.

The *Being a Reader* program's academic strands provide students with a wide range of essential early literacy experiences. These strands combine to inspire the students' love of reading, allow them to move at their own pace along a continuum of reading development, build their confidence, and establish their sense of identity as readers. In addition to Small-group Reading, the program includes four types of whole-class lessons: Shared Reading (grades K–1), Independent Work (grades K–2), Handwriting (grades K–1), and Word Study (grade 2). For more information about the *Being a Reader* program, see the Introduction in your grade-level *Being a Reader Teacher's Manual*.

- **Shared Reading (K–1).** In Shared Reading, the teacher reads and rereads carefully selected large-format texts with the whole class. The teacher models effective reading behaviors and strategies, and invites the students to be involved. Shared Reading offers a supportive context for young learners to develop a delight in reading and an understanding of their ability to interact with texts.

- **Independent Work (K–2).** During Independent Work, students take responsibility for their learning and behavior by working independently on meaningful literacy activities while the teacher instructs small groups or individuals. Students have the opportunity to be autonomous as they practice procedures, internalize expectations, monitor their own behavior, and make decisions about how to work independently.

- **Handwriting (K–1).** In the first weeks of the year, the lessons focus on hand and finger strengthening, pencil grip, posture, and paper placement. Then, as the students begin independent work rotations, the lessons begin to focus on letter formation. Teacher-led Handwriting lessons occur once a week throughout kindergarten and for the first half of grade 1.

- **Word Study (2).** Word Study lessons focus on developing the strategies students can use to decode polysyllabic words. Word Study develops the students' understanding of how words are constructed and engages them in examining patterns and similarities in words. This instruction also helps the students develop curiosity about the structure of words that will benefit them in later grades.

Small-group Reading at a Glance

In the Small-group Reading strand of the *Being a Reader* program, the students work with you in differentiated groups to become strategic readers. The small-group reading sets allow students to move at their own pace in their reading development. You will carefully match the students with texts at their assessed reading levels and provide instruction to address their differing needs. See "Placement Assessment" on page xx.

During small-group instruction, you will strive to understand how each student learns and where the student excels and/or needs more support. Working with students in small groups allows you to efficiently match the needs of individual readers as you teach strategies and skills for the students to apply to their independent reading. Small groups of students naturally build community as they work together on similar goals and learn from one another.

There are two phases of small-group sets: one for emerging readers (Sets 1–5) and one for developing readers (Sets 6–12).

SMALL-GROUP READING SETS 1–5 (EMERGING READERS)

Small-group reading instruction for emerging readers was developed for students who are just beginning to grasp letter-sound relationships and the conventions of written English. The goal for these sets is to quickly and efficiently teach foundational skills in the context of reading for comprehension and develop the students' understanding of themselves as readers. In these sets, the students read books that correspond to a scope and sequence of phonics and high-frequency word instruction. The books were developed by the Center for the Collaborative Classroom with careful attention to natural-sounding language, plot and character development, a variety of appropriate fiction and nonfiction topics, and high-quality illustrations. Lessons that accompany these books focus on phonological awareness, concepts of print, phonics/decoding, and high-frequency word recognition. By the end of Set 5, the students will have mastered single-syllable phonics, acquired many high-frequency words, and been introduced to polysyllabic decoding. They will also have had many experiences using reading strategies informally to understand text.

SMALL-GROUP READING SETS 6–12 (DEVELOPING READERS)

Small-group reading instruction for developing readers teaches explicit strategies with the goal of having the students apply the strategies to their independent reading. These students are ready to practice, apply, and expand on a wide array of reading tools, building upon the decoding instruction and informal strategy instruction introduced in Sets 1–5. Strategies and texts taught in each set are appropriate for students at that stage of reading development and become more complex as the students advance. In earlier sets, you will provide more modeling and support for a strategy, while in later sets, you will guide the students to use the strategy more independently and in deeper ways.

Understanding Small-group Reading Sets 1–5

This *Small-group Reading Teacher's Manual* focuses on the phase of small-group instruction intended for emerging readers.

Many factors contribute to students becoming confident, competent readers, including oral fluency, word-recognition strategies, comprehension, and a love of reading. Small-group Reading Sets 1-5 focus on important parts of learning—phonological awareness, concepts of print, decoding, high-frequency words, and comprehension.

Beginning readers learn that spelling-sound knowledge is vital to decoding text. They come to realize that spoken words are made up of sound units (phonemes) and that the spellings they see on a page correspond with these phonemes. Once the students learn how to connect letters and sounds, they can efficiently read many words. Sets 1-5 build the foundation for reading through systematic instruction in phonological awareness, spelling-sound decoding, and high-frequency words. As the students learn to read accurately and automatically, the students also learn that understanding what they are reading is paramount.

Design Features of Small-group Reading Sets 1–5

Small-group Reading Sets 1-5 differ from more traditional approaches to small-group instruction in some important ways:

- In Small-group Reading, instruction is explicit and systematic.

- Small-group Reading lessons are fully articulated and support you to be thoroughly prepared to lead the group. The step-by-step instruction frees you to focus on the students and their reading.

- When students are correctly placed in the appropriate set, they receive the instruction they need. Students do not unnecessarily repeat instruction or receive instruction beyond what they are ready for.

- The books the students read were developed to correspond to the scope and sequence of phonics and high-frequency word instruction. These books provide opportunities to engage in comprehension work within and beyond the text.

Goals for Emerging Readers

The primary goals of Small-group Reading Sets 1–5 are for the students to:

- Receive explicit, systematic instruction in phonological awareness, spelling-sounds, and high-frequency words

- Comprehend what they read

- Cultivate a love of reading

- Learn to read well independently

- Receive individualized instruction

- Read a variety of high-quality books

Elements of Instruction

Instruction for emerging readers is guided by a scope and sequence of phonological awareness, phonics, and high-frequency words. Spelling-sounds and high-frequency words are taught in order of utility, with the goal of quickly preparing students to start reading books. Success in reading is a strong motivator for young readers. As the books become more challenging, reading strategies such as retelling, identifying characters' feelings, and making connections are informally introduced.

Emerging readers learn at different paces, and the small-group lessons provide opportunities for reteaching to slow the pace of instruction as necessary. At the same time, some readers make sudden gains in their decoding ability at different times. These students may be able to move ahead in the instructional sequence. For the complete scope and sequence for Sets 1–5 and Sets 6–12, see Appendix D, "Scope and Sequence" in your grade-level whole-class *Teacher's Manual*, or visit the General Resources section of the CCC Learning Hub (ccclearninghub.org).

PHONOLOGICAL AWARENESS

Phonological awareness is the awareness that words are made up of sounds. The ability to hear the different sounds that make up a word is critical for both reading and spelling. Through a variety of oral activities, the students identify the phonemes in words. Basic blending (/mmăănn/ into *man*) and segmenting (*man* into /mm/ /ăă/ /nn/) activities lead to identifying first, last, and middle sounds and finally dropping and substituting sounds. Oral phonological awareness activities appear in every week.

SPELLING-SOUNDS

Explicit, systematic instruction ensures that the students build their knowledge of spelling-sound relationships by applying them to reading words in isolation (in word lists) and in books. Spelling-sounds are introduced gradually, with ample time for practice. Decodable word lists often include challenging words from the week's book. This provides the students with opportunities to read words with teacher support before they encounter them when reading to themselves. Once a week, the students review spelling-sounds in isolation using the sound card review deck. This helps to solidify their knowledge and allows you to evaluate the students' mastery of the spelling-sounds. To hear the recommended pronunciation for sounds, see the video "Pronunciation Guide" on the CCC Learning Hub.

SOUND SORTS

Sorting independently reinforces spelling-sound knowledge and provides review on days when the small group does not meet. The students first work with pictures that show familiar objects (such as the sun). The students sort pictures according to the first, last, or middle sound in the word (/ss/ /ŭŭ/ /nn/), which builds phonological awareness. In later sets, the students sort words based on the week's spelling-sound instruction. The word sorts are the foundation for word study in later grades.

POLYSYLLABIC WORDS

Reading polysyllabic words requires students to use different strategies than simple left-to-right decoding. At this stage of reading development, students begin to read words in syllables or word parts rather than letter by letter. As early as Set 4, the students begin to read two-syllable words that include inflectional endings. In Set 5, the students are introduced to strategies for reading polysyllabic words and begin to develop the word analysis skills that will allow them to tackle easy-to-read trade books (books at level J of the *Fountas & Pinnell Text Level Gradient*™ or level 18 of the *Developmental Reading Assessment*® [DRA]). As the students are ready, you may encourage them to add easy-to-read books to their toolboxes for independent reading.

HIGH-FREQUENCY WORDS

read + spell sightwords

A repertoire of high-frequency words supports students' automaticity in reading connected text. After you introduce each word, the students read and spell it, which focuses the students' attention on the left-to-right sequence of letters. High-frequency words are reviewed daily and are added cumulatively to the weekly books. Word cards that can be added to the class word wall are provided, as well as a "Word Bank" that the students can use for reference. Find the "Word Bank" in the General Resources section of the CCC Learning Hub (ccclearninghub.org).

FLUENCY

Fluency is more than reading rate. It is the ability to read text accurately, automatically, and with expression. Students who read fluently have made the leap from word-by-word processing of text to smoother, more natural-sounding reading (when reading aloud and when reading silently to themselves). When students read fluently, they are able to focus on the meaning of what they are reading rather than on reading individual words.

Instruction and practice with spelling-sound correspondences and high-frequency words builds the accuracy and automaticity needed to read with expression and proper phrasing. Emerging readers at first read haltingly, word by word. But beginning in Set 4 or 5, you will notice the students starting to read in phrases. At this point, the students will be paying increasing attention to comprehension. Students who still struggle with phrasing after completing Set 5 can go on to Set 6, which focuses on fluency, while those who are reading with prosody continue to Set 7 or 8.

COMPREHENSION

The purpose of teaching spelling-sound correspondences, high-frequency words, and strategies for reading polysyllabic words is to facilitate comprehension. Students who read accurately and with automaticity and prosody are able to direct most of their attention to understanding what they read. Sets 1 and 2 focus on establishing accuracy and automaticity in the context of reading fiction and nonfiction with plots and topics that are readily accessible to the students. Repeated rereading in Small-group Reading lessons and during independent work time develops fluency. The students read and discuss books during every Small-group Reading lesson. Discussion questions beginning in Set 3 start to informally address some of the comprehension strategies that will appear in later sets, such as using illustrations to support comprehension, using text features, and understanding how characters change during a story.

GUIDED SPELLING

In each Guided Spelling lesson, the students spell decodable words and high-frequency words with teacher support. Spelling practice coordinated with on-level reading strengthens both reading (decoding) and spelling (encoding). The purpose of Guided Spelling is to support the students in being strategic spellers rather than to test their knowledge of individual words. It is an opportunity for the students to apply their growing knowledge to writing.

Texts for Emerging Readers (Sets 1–5)

The books provided for Sets 1–5 have been carefully written and illustrated to provide engaging reading experiences within the scope and sequence of Small-group Reading. The books are attractive, appealing, and designed for success.

Each set includes a balance of fiction and nonfiction texts. Nonfiction becomes more prevalent in later sets.

The books in Set 1 make full use of high-frequency words and a few spelling-sound relationships. The books taught in the first two weeks use only high-frequency words, allowing the students to start reading real books immediately. Simple consonant-vowel-consonant (CVC) words are added as soon as the students learn their first vowel spelling-sound.

The books in Set 2 include nonfiction about single topics, such as sled dogs and animal homes. The fiction books focus on single events.

Nonfiction books in Set 3 include information about single topics, such as skunks and making jam. The plots of fiction books are more complex here than in previous sets. Comprehension questions begin to informally address topics taught in depth in later sets, such as using illustrations to confirm what one reads, identifying characters' feelings and how they change, and making inferences.

Nonfiction books in Set 4 include less familiar topics, such as life in a Native American plains tribe. The more complex plots of fiction books require the students to make inferences. Comprehension questions continue to informally address topics taught in depth in later lessons.

Set 5 includes mostly nonfiction books featuring new topics with more complex content, such as why we have night and day on Earth and how glaciers shape the planet. Comprehension questions informally address topics taught in depth in later sets, such as making connections between texts and identifying information that is learned from a book. The students in Set 5 are likely to be able to add easy-to-read trade books to their repertoire. Abundant reading with high levels of accuracy develops fluency, comprehension, and vocabulary. The students at this stage of development will benefit from reading a large variety of books at their appropriate reading levels.

Teaching Small-group Reading Sets 1–5

How Sets 1-5 Are Organized

Each set features between 12 and 21 books. There are three lessons associated with each main book, plus an additional Reteaching text provided for every other week. Lessons are designed to take approximately 15 minutes in kindergarten. In grade 1, Guided Spelling takes an additional 5 minutes. Each week of instruction follows a similar outline, with some variation in later sets. Using a familiar lesson structure allows the students to focus on new content.

The steps on Days 1 and 2 follow a similar sequence:

- **Phonological Awareness.** The lessons begin with an oral phonological awareness activity. Blending and segmenting are emphasized in early sets, and more sophisticated activities are emphasized in later sets. These activities become less frequent on Day 2 beginning in Set 5.

- **Introduce the Spelling-Sound.** A spelling-sound is introduced through modeling and practice.

- **Blend Decodable Words.** The students practice blending words in a list. Many of the words are selected from the week's new book. Once the students are reading two-syllable words, this step is called "Read Decodable Words," because the students begin to read by syllable rather than by blending individual sounds.

- **Introduce the Sound Sort.** On Day 2, a new sound sort is included in the instruction.

- **Introduce the High-frequency Word.** A word is introduced through reading and spelling.

- **Review High-frequency Words.** Words are reviewed using handheld cards.

- **Read or Reread.** On Day 1, the students reread the previous week's book. On Day 2, they read a new book. Comprehension questions are provided.

- **Guided Spelling (for grade 1 students).** The students are guided to spell two decodable words and then write one high-frequency word.

On Day 3, the format is modified to allow more time for review, reading, and discussion. No new sounds or words are introduced.

- **Phonological Awareness.** The Day 3 lesson usually begins with an oral phonological awareness activity. These activities become less frequent on Day 3 beginning in Set 4.

- **Review Spelling-Sounds.** Spelling-sounds are reviewed using handheld cards.

- **Review High-frequency Words.** Words are reviewed using handheld cards.

- **Reread.** The students reread the Day 2 book.

- **Check Comprehension and Reflect.** The students answer comprehension questions and discuss what they have read.

- **Guided Spelling (for grade 1 students).** The students are guided to spell the words in a sentence, including capitalization and ending punctuation.

Planning and Teaching the Lessons

SET OVERVIEW

To prepare to teach each set, begin by reading the Set introduction. The Set introduction describes the readers at that level, the characteristics of the texts in the set, and the focuses of the instruction.

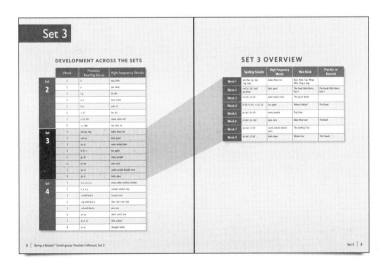

The Development Across the Sets table provides a context for the material covered in each set by listing material covered in the previous and subsequent sets. The table can serve as a reminder of what spelling-sounds and high-frequency words the group has recently covered, as well as a preview of what is covered in the next set.

SCHEDULING LESSONS

Small-group Reading was developed to be used in conjunction with independent work, enabling you to meet with four small groups, three times per week each (in 12 total instructional sessions). If you have more than four groups or find that you want to meet with some groups more often than others, you can schedule your groups into the 12 sessions according to your students' needs.

To schedule your small-group instruction, write the instructional lessons and any Reteaching lessons you plan to teach each group on the "Small-group Reading Two-week Planner." Visit the CCC Learning Hub (ccclearninghub.org) to access and print the planner.

Date: January 10-14

	Monday	Tuesday	Wednesday	Thursday	Friday
Group 1		Set 1, Week 1, Day 1		Set 1, Week 1, Day 2	Set 1, Week 1, Day 3
Group 2	Set 1 Week 8, Day 3			Set 2, Week 1, Day 1	Set 2, Week 1, Day 2
Group 3	Set 3, Week 1, Day 2	Set 3, Week 1, Day 3			Set 3, Week 2, Day 1
Group 4	Set 4, Week 5, Day 2	Set 4, Week 5, Day 3		Set 4, Week 6, Day 1	

Date: January 17-21

	Monday	Tuesday	Wednesday	Thursday	Friday
Group 1		Set 1, Week 2, Day 1		Set 1, Week 2, Day 2	Set 1, Week 2, Day 3
Group 2	Set 2 Week 1, Day 3			Set 2, Week 2, Day 1	Set 2, Week 2, Day 2
Group 3	Set 3, Week 2, Day 2	Set 3, Week 2, Day 3			Set 3, Week 3, Day 1
Group 4	Set 4, Week 6, Day 2	Set 4, Week 6, Day 3		Set 4, Week 7, Day 1	

ENTRY-POINT WEEKS

Because students may enter the Small-group Reading lessons at varying points along the instructional continuum, you may have students who are beginning instruction with the first week in a set. The activities in Week 1 of each set are written out completely for groups that are beginning instruction. If you are teaching an entry-point lesson, consider budgeting more time for modeling than you normally would.

If your group is continuing from the previous week, you will not need to repeat the activity introductions in Week 1 of the new set; simply remind the students of your expectations. Beginning in Week 2, instruction is abbreviated unless a new activity is being introduced.

 *To prep*

PREPARING THE DAILY LESSONS

To prepare to teach a set of lessons, begin by reading the lessons and thinking about how to tailor them to meet the students' needs. The Resources list specifies the books, assessment forms, and reproducibles that will be used throughout the set of lessons. The Online Resources list indicates all of the materials that are available digitally on the CCC Learning Hub (ccclearninghub.org). The Overview lists the academic goals and alerts you to any advance preparation needed for each lesson.

Before teaching a set of lessons:

- Read each lesson carefully, including Teacher Notes and Support Notes.

- Read any book that is new to the students. Review the concepts and vocabulary to be introduced before the students read, and anticipate whether any students will need additional support with background knowledge or vocabulary. We provide suggestions in each book introduction, but you may decide to provide additional support.

- Make any preparations specified in the "Do Ahead" section of the Overview.

- Gather the necessary materials and organize them near your small-group area.

- Review the "ELL Support" feature in the Overview. This feature helps you anticipate spelling-sounds that may be challenging for students depending on their language backgrounds.

GUIDED SPELLING FOR GRADE 1 STUDENTS *use white 8ds*

In Guided Spelling lessons on Days 1 and 2, the students spell two decodable words and one high-frequency word with your support. On Day 3, they write a sentence as you support them in the conventions of sentence writing, including capitalization and punctuation. Guided Spelling sessions are intended for grade 1 students, but kindergarten students may also benefit from Guided Spelling instruction if time is available.

Guided Spelling lessons should take approximately 5 minutes. For each word, say the word, have the students say it, and then support them as they spell. For decodable words, refer to the "Spelling Support" section for specific suggestions to help you guide the students. For high-frequency words, allow the students to use the word wall or their personal "Word Bank" for support as needed. Find the "Word Bank" in the General Resources section of the CCC Learning Hub (ccclearninghub.org).

RETEACHING

Every two weeks, an assessment note alerts you to consider slowing the pace of instruction for the group by reteaching content. A new book is provided for application of the spelling-sounds and high-frequency words taught during the previous two weeks. Use the same three-day pattern laid out for regular weeks, dividing spelling-sounds and high-frequency words to be taught over the first two days, introducing the new book on Day 2, and following up with review, rereading, and discussion on Day 3. Some groups, especially in Set 1, may need two Reteaching weeks rather than one. Students who do not need reteaching can use the reteaching book for independent reading.

Assessments

PLACEMENT ASSESSMENT

A placement assessment for Sets 1–5 will help you determine the appropriate small group in which to place each student, and which set the group will begin in. Once you have assessed the students and grouped them, instruction can begin. The placement assessment and instructions for administering it can be found in the *Assessment Resource Book*.

Forming Small Groups

You will form differentiated small groups after finishing beginning-of-the-year placement assessments and setting the foundation for independent work. In kindergarten, it is likely that some students will be ready for small-group instruction earlier in the year than other students. For students who are not ready for reading instruction, use the suggestions in Appendix E, "Letter-name Instruction," in your grade-level whole-class *Being a Reader Teacher's Manual* to teach letter names. For information on assessment, forming and managing reading groups, and monitoring student progress, see the *Assessment Resource Book*.

FORMATIVE ASSESSMENTS

Individual Reading Observation

Beginning in Set 3, the Individual Reading Observation will give you the opportunity to listen to and observe individual students as they read. An Individual Reading Observation Note will appear every two weeks on Day 3. You can record your observations about each student on an "Individual Reading Observation" sheet (IR), which should be printed out before you begin teaching each set. For information on the "Individual Reading Observation" sheet, see the *Assessment Resource Book*. The sheets are also available on the CCC Learning Hub (ccclearninghub.org). Alternatively, you can use the CCC ClassView™ assessment app to electronically record data on a record sheet. For more information, see "CCC ClassView App" in the Introduction of your grade-level *Teacher's Manual*. You can also access the CCC ClassView app directly (classview.org).

Group Progress Assessment

The Group Progress Assessment will give you the opportunity to observe the group as they practice strategies. A Group Progress Assessment Note will appear every four weeks, on Day 3. Each Group Progress Assessment Note has a corresponding "Group Progress Assessment" sheet (GA), which should be printed out before you begin teaching the lesson. The sheet includes questions that you can ask yourself to focus your observations as well as suggestions for how to proceed with the instruction based on those observations. For information on the "Group Progress Assessment" sheet, see the *Assessment Resource Book*. You will find copies of "Group Progress Assessment" sheets in the *Assessment Resource Book*. The sheets are also available on the CCC Learning Hub (ccclearninghub.org). Alternatively, you can use the CCC ClassView app to electronically record data on a record sheet. For more information, see "CCC ClassView App" in the Introduction of your grade-level *Teacher's Manual*.

SUMMATIVE ASSESSMENTS

The Mastery Tests will allow you to monitor the progress of individual students. A Mastery Test Assessment Note will appear every four weeks, on Day 3. Each Mastery Test has a "Mastery Test" record (MT) and a corresponding "Mastery Test Student Card" (SC) for the students to read from. Suggestions for reteaching as needed are provided with each Mastery Test Assessment Note. The students who master material in a set should move directly into Week 1 of the next set. You will find the Mastery Tests in the *Assessment Resource Book*. The sheets are also available on the CCC Learning Hub (ccclearninghub.org). Alternatively, you can use the CCC ClassView app to electronically record data on a record sheet. For more information, see "CCC ClassView App" in the Introduction of your grade-level *Teacher's Manual*.

Tips for Managing Small-group Reading in Your Classroom

Small-group Reading lessons assume students' familiarity with some basic procedures, cooperative structures, and facilitation techniques.

ROOM ARRANGEMENT AND MATERIALS

For Small-group Reading, the students should sit at a table facing you, close enough to see the cards and wipe-off board. Individual wipe-off boards are used by the grade 1 students during Guided Spelling. The students participating in Guided Spelling should be seated so that they can easily refer to the high-frequency word wall.

You may want to post your "Small-group Reading Two-week Planner" next to the small-group table so that you know which groups you will see each day. When you signal for the students to switch tasks, ask the students in the next small group to sit at the small-group reading table. Visit the CCC Learning Hub (ccclearninghub.org) to access and print the planner.

The students may need to practice moving quickly and quietly to the small-group reading area. Consider beginning each instructional session by asking questions that help the students take responsibility for the gathering procedure, such as "How did you do with coming to the small-group reading area quickly and quietly?"

Since the students carry their toolboxes during independent work rotations, they will bring their toolboxes with them to the small-group reading table. The students store their books and bags containing sound sorts in their toolboxes.

Special Considerations

 ## Support for English Language Learners

Small-group Reading in the *Being a Reader* program is designed to be accessible to all students. Special attention was given to particular challenges for English Language Learners. An "ELL Support" feature before each set of lessons alerts you to pronunciation and language transfer issues that may arise during the lessons. Additionally, ELL Notes at point of use provide information that can be included in the lessons, including vocabulary support and background knowledge needed to comprehend the weekly books. For more information about how the program supports English Language Learners, see "Supporting English Language Learners" in the Introduction of your grade-level *Being a Reader Teacher's Manual*.

Lessons

Set 3

Set 3 readers have mastered short vowels and single consonants. They are comfortable reading consonant-vowel-consonant (CVC) words, although they may read slowly, word by word. Their increasing facility with one-syllable and high-frequency words allows them to attend more to the content of what they are reading. Set 3 lessons introduce consonant blends and inflectional endings. By the end of the set, the students may begin to read more smoothly by grouping words together.

Nonfiction books in this set include information about single topics, such as skunks and making jam. The plots of fiction stories are more complex than those in previous sets. Comprehension questions begin to informally address topics taught in depth in later sets, such as using illustrations to confirm what one reads, identifying characters' feelings and how they change, and making inferences.

Set 3

DEVELOPMENT ACROSS THE SETS

	Week	Phonics/ Reading Focus	High-frequency Words
Set 2	1	b	was, little
	2	p	put, what
	3	l, g	do, like
	4	e, w	have, home
	5	th, y	said, of
	6	v, sh	her, his
	7	x, ch, tch	some, come, out
	8	z, j, dge	say, says, so
Set 3	1	wh, ng, -ing	make, there, be
	2	-ed, qu	look, good
	3	sn, st	want, water, from
	4	fl, fr, -s	for, again
	5	gr, dr	many, people
	6	pl, sm	your, very
	7	sp, cl	could, would, should, were
	8	sk, sl	both, does
Set 4	1	a_e, i_e, e_e	every, other, mother, brother
	2	o_e, u_e	woman, women, boy
	3	-s with final e	toward, over
	4	-ing with final e	their, old, cold, told
	5	-ed with final e	one, two
	6	ee, ea	don't, won't, too
	7	er, ir, ur	who, school
	8	ar, or	thought, father

SET 3 OVERVIEW

	Spelling-Sounds	High-frequency Words	New Book	Practice or Reteach
Week 1	wh /hw/, ng /ng/, -ing /ing/	make, there, be	Buzz, Hum, Tap, Whap, Whiz, Ding-a-ling	
Week 2	-ed /t/, /d/, /əd/; qu /khw/	look, good	The Good Little Ducks, Part 1	The Good Little Ducks, Part 2
Week 3	sn /sn/, st /st/	want, water, from	The Jug of Water	
Week 4	fl /fl/; fr /fr/; -s /s/, /z/	for, again	Where Is Mom?	The Skunk
Week 5	gr /gr/, dr /dr/	many, people	Drip Drop	
Week 6	pl /pl/, sm /sm/	your, very	Make Plum Jam	The Band
Week 7	sp /sp/, cl /kl/	could, would, should, were	The Spelling Test	
Week 8	sk /sk/, sl /sl/	both, does	Winter Fun	The Clowns

RESOURCES

New

Buzz, Hum, Tap, Whap, Whiz, Ding-a-ling

by Corinn Kintz

Revisit (with continuing students)

On the Job

by Amy Helfer

Assessment Resource Book

- Week 1 assessment

Sound Cards

- *wh* /hw/
- *ng* /ng/
- *_ing* /ing/

High-frequency Word Cards

- *make*
- *there*
- *be*

Wipe-off Boards

 ## Online Resources

Visit the CCC Learning Hub (ccclearninghub.org) to find your online resources for this week.

Assessment Form

- "Individual Reading Observation" sheet (IR1)

Reproducible

- "Set 3, Week 1 Sort" (BLM1)

OVERVIEW

Spelling-Sound Focus	High-frequency Words
▪ wh /hw/ (whale)	▪ make
▪ ng /ng/	▪ there
▪ inflectional ending -ing	▪ be

[handwritten notes: Prep / -Find word cards / make / there / be / wh / ng / ing / go online to find sorts / -get sound cards]

① DO AHEAD

✓ Prior to Day 1, add high-frequency word cards for *make, there*, and *be* to the word wall if they are not already displayed.

✓ Prior to Day 2, visit the CCC Learning Hub (ccclearninghub.org) to access and print "Set 3, Week 1 Sort" (BLM1). Make a copy for each student in the group, plus two. Cut apart the pictures on each sheet (keeping one copy intact) to create a set of sorting pictures for beginning sounds /j/ and /ch/ for each student in the group and one for yourself. Place each set of pictures in a resealable plastic bag.

✓ Prior to Day 3, if your group is continuing from Set 2, add the sound cards for *wh*, *ng*, and *_ing* to the sound card review deck. If your group is beginning with this lesson, use the sound cards for *wh*, *ng*, and *_ing* to start the review deck.

✓ Prior to Day 3, make a group set of the "Individual Reading Observation" sheet (IR1); see page 149 of the *Assessment Resource Book* or the CCC Learning Hub. Make a copy for each student in the group. You will use the observation sheets throughout this set of lessons.

[handwritten notes: # review / are / where / here / her]

🌐 ELL SUPPORT

▪ wh

Speakers of Spanish, Cantonese, Vietnamese, and Hmong may be unfamiliar with the sound /hw/. Have the students listen to and repeat words that begin with this sound. Emphasize the mouth position for the beginning sound as you say it and have the students repeat after you.

(continues)

🌐 ELL SUPPORT *(continued)*

• ng

When you introduce *ng* to Spanish-speaking students, help them make the connection between the English sounds and the sounds that occur at syllable junctures in Spanish words. Explain that the sound /ng/ is like the sound they hear in the middle of the words *bilingüe* (bee-LEEN-gway), "bilingual," and *tengo* (TAYN-goh), "I have."

• there

English Language Learners often have difficulty distinguishing and producing *r*-controlled vowels. When you introduce *there*, you may wish to review the words *are*, *where*, *here*, and *her*. Write these words where the students can see them, and pair each with a mnemonic picture to cue the vowel sound (such as pictures of a car, pear, deer, and bird). Call on the students to quickly identify the words in random sequence. For example: *are* (car), *where* and *there* (pear), *here* (deer), *her* (bird).

In this lesson, the students:

- Practice oral blending
- Learn the spelling-sound *wh* /hw/
- Read decodable words
- Learn the high-frequency words *make* and *there*
- Review high-frequency words
- Read a familiar book (continuing students)

ABOUT ENTRY-POINT LESSONS

Because students may enter the Small-group Reading lessons at varying points along the instructional continuum, you may have students who are beginning instruction with this lesson or who are continuing from Set 2. Each activity in this week is written out completely for groups that are beginning instruction with this lesson.

If your group is continuing from the previous week, you will not need to repeat the activity introductions in this lesson; simply remind the students of your expectations for the procedures.

1 Gather and Get Ready

Explain that during Small-group Reading the students will learn new sounds and words, read books, and talk about their reading.

2 Phonological Awareness: Oral Blending

Explain that you will say the sounds in a word, and then the students will put the sounds together to make the word. Model the procedure, using the word *whiz*. Slowly and clearly, say the sounds three times, drawing out the sounds as you say them: /hwĭĭzz/. Clap softly as you say each sound. Then blend the sounds more quickly to make the word. Brush your hands past each other as you say the word. Slowly say the sounds one more time: /hwĭĭzz/. Have the students repeat by drawing out the sounds and then blending them to say the word. Repeat the procedure to practice blending a second word, such as *jam*.

Blend out loud

Materials

- (For continuing students) Teacher and student copies of *On the Job* from Set 2, Week 8
- Wipe-off board, dry-erase marker, and tissue or cloth
- High-frequency word card for *make*
- High-frequency word card for *there*
- High-frequency word card review deck
- (Optional, for students beginning with this lesson) Student copies of *A Bad Fox* from Set 2, Week 8
- (For Guided Spelling) Wipe-off board, dry-erase marker, and tissue or cloth for each student

Teacher Note

If the students are familiar with the oral blending routine, you do not need to model it here. Instead, simply go to the word list on the next page and remind the students of your expectations for the procedure.

Blending Support

For blending activities, use continuous blending, drawing out the sounds without leaving pauses between them (for example, /hwĭzz/, not /hw/ /ĭ/ /zz/). Model this for the students and have them also use continuous blending. In contrast, when segmenting, leave a very short pause between sounds.

If the students have difficulty blending, you might use a visual aid. Draw three blanks side by side on a wipe-off board and point to each blank as you say each sound again slowly. Sweep under all three blanks as you say the word. Then have the students say the sounds as you point to the blanks and say the word as you sweep under them.

Have the students blend each of the words that follow. Say the phonemes using continuous blending and have the students repeat. Remember to clap softly as you say each sound and then brush your hands past each other as the students say the word.

/hwĭĭff/	whiff
/hwĕĕnn/	when
/hwăămm/	wham
/hwĭĭch/	which
/hwĭĭp/	whip
/hwĭĭmm/	whim

3 Introduce the Spelling-Sound *wh* /hw/

Explain that today's sound is /hw/, and have the students say the sound. Point to the alphabet wall card for *wh*. Tell the students that the picture of the whale will help them remember the sound /hw/ because the word *whale* begins with the sound /hw/. Write *wh* on the lined side of your wipe-off board, point to the spelling, and say the letter names. Tell the students that the spelling *w-h* stands for the sound /hw/. Have the students repeat the sound as you point to the spelling. Then have the students each trace the spelling *w-h* on the table in front of them with one finger as they say /hw/.

4 Read Decodable Words

Tell the students that they will read words that use spellings they know. Explain that you will write some words, and the students will read them. Some of the words can be sounded out, and some have base words that can be sounded out, plus inflectional endings. Explain that the students will have to recognize the endings *i-n-g* and *e-d* when they come to them.

Explain that to read the list, you will point to a word and wait to give the students a chance to read the word quietly to themselves. Then, all the students will read the word aloud together. Model with the word *whizzing*. Write *whizzing* on your wipe-off board, point to the left of the word, pause, and then sweep under the word as the students read it. You may wish to establish a cue, such as "Read," to signal the group when

Teacher Note

The sound /hw/ is disappearing from many regional dialects. The students may say /hw/ as /w/ when they are reading words.

Teacher Note

This is the first time students are asked to read decodable words, rather than blend them. Provide the full instruction and modeling, even if this group is continuing instruction from Set 2.

Teacher Note

Many of the words in the Read Decodable Words activities are selected from the books students read on Day 2.

to read. If necessary, use the tips in the Decoding Support note below to support the students.

Write the following words on your wipe-off board:

when	which
edge	whap
buzzing	mixing

Point to the left of *when* and sweep under it as the students read it. Follow the same procedure for the remaining words on the list.

Decoding Support

If the students struggle to blend decodable words, support them by saying each sound with them while you point to each spelling. Then have the students blend the sounds to read the word. For words with inflectional endings, cover the ending (and any doubled letters) and have the students read the base word in isolation before reading the whole word.

5 Introduce the High-frequency Words *Make* and *There*

make	"I will make a birthday card for my sister."
there	"Look over there."

Tell the students that *high-frequency words* are words they will see again and again in their reading. Explain that recognizing these words will help them read stories. Tell the students that today they will learn two new high-frequency words, and explain that the first new word is *make*. Say *make*. Use *make* in a sentence. ("I will make a birthday card for my sister.") Show the high-frequency word card for *make*, point to the word, and say it as you sweep under it. Consider establishing a signal, such as pointing to the first letter of the word or saying "Read," to support the students in reading the words chorally.

Tell the students that when they are learning a new high-frequency word, they will practice by reading the word and spelling it. Have the students chorally read *make* and then spell *make* as you point to each letter. Then have them read, spell, and read the word again.

Point to *make* on the word wall.

Repeat the procedure for the high-frequency word *there*, using an example sentence such as "Look over there." Point to *there* on the word wall. Use the word cards for *make* and *there* to begin the high-frequency word card review deck.

6 Review High-frequency Words

Tell the students that on small-group reading days they will review some of the words they have already learned by reading them from cards. Explain that they will read each word, spell it, and then read it again. Model the procedure, using *make*. Hold up the card, point to the left of

Teacher Note

You may wish to write the homophones *there*, *their*, and *they're* on your wipe-off board. Read each word aloud as you point to it. Explain to the students that these three words sound the same but have different meanings: *There* means "a place." ("Please go over there.") *Their* means "belonging to them." ("I am their teacher.") *They're* is a shorter way to say *they are*. ("They're sitting at the table.") Tell the students that they can usually figure out which word is meant by listening to the sentence the word is in. As you point to it, review that the word they are learning today is *there*, as in "The books are there on the shelf."

Teacher Note

If your group is continuing from Set 2, add the word cards for *make* and *there* to the high-frequency word card review deck.

Teacher Note

If your group is continuing from Set 2, retain only the cards for the words the students do not know well in the review deck.

the word, and read it aloud. Then point under each letter as you say each letter name. Finally, read the word again as you sweep under it.

Teacher Note

If the students struggle to read a high-frequency word, say the word and then have the students read it and spell it.

Have the students practice reading, spelling, and then rereading the word *make*. Practice again, using the word *there*. To review previously introduced high-frequency words with continuing students, show each word in the review deck and have the students read it, spell it, and read it again.

Teacher Note

The rereading step is intended for students who are continuing instruction from Set 2. If your group is beginning instruction with this lesson, you may wish to have the students read *A Bad Fox* using the preteaching words and comprehension questions from Set 2, Week 8.

7 Reread *On the Job* with Continuing Students

Have the students take the book *On the Job* from their toolboxes. Tell the students that they will reread this book today. Read the title with the students and ask:

Q *What do you remember about this book?*

Have a few volunteers share their thinking with the group. Then have the students read the book in quiet voices.

Monitor the students as they read, and support any student who struggles. When all the students have finished reading, collect the books or have the students return their books to their toolboxes.

Teacher Note

Guided Spelling is an optional component intended for grade 1 students. In every Guided Spelling lesson, the students will need wipe-off boards, dry-erase markers, and tissue or cloth.

If your group is continuing, simply support the students in writing the words as you did in previous lessons. See "Spelling Support" at the end of the Guided Spelling section.

GUIDED SPELLING

which	"Which of our books is your favorite?"
when	"When is your birthday?"
says	"Kenji says he likes to read about airplanes."

Distribute wipe-off boards, dry-erase markers, and tissues or pieces of soft cloth to the students. Tell them that they will use these boards throughout the year to write letters, words, and sentences, and remind them of your expectations for use.

Tell the students that when they write words, they will use the side of the board with lines. Explain that they will write each word you say, check their word, and then erase the word.

Teacher Note

For segmenting activities, draw out the sounds leaving a very short pause between them (/sh/ /ĭ/ /p/, not /shĭĭp/).

Explain to the students that when they are spelling, it is often helpful to *segment* words, or say all the sounds in the word before they write. Model how to segment a word, using the word *ship*. Say the word normally: *ship*; then say it again, drawing out the sounds: /shh/ /ĭĭ/ /p/. Finally, say each individual sound: /sh/ /ĭ/ /p/. Clap softly as you say each sound. Tell the students that you clapped three times as you said the sounds, so there are three sounds in the word. Have the students practice with the word *judge*. Have the students say *judge* and then segment *judge*, clapping softly on each sound.

Say *which*. Use *which* in a sentence. ("Which of our books is your favorite?") Have the students segment *which*, clapping softly as they say each sound. Then ask them how many sounds they hear in the word. Encourage the students to pay attention to all the sounds in the word as they write the word on the lined side of their wipe-off board. Remind them that in *which*, the sound /hw/ is spelled *w-h* and tell them that the sound /ch/ is spelled *c-h*. Have the students write *which*.

When all the students have finished writing, write *which* on your own wipe-off board.

Tell the students that they will check their work by comparing the word they wrote to the one you wrote. Explain that they will compare each letter in the word to make sure all the letters are there and that they are in the same order. Model this by writing *whech* on your wipe-off board and then comparing each letter to *which*. When you get to the mistake, tell the students that you see that you made a mistake; then change *e* to *i*. Have the students check their work and erase and correct any mistakes they find.

Have the students erase *which*.

Say *when*. Use *when* in a sentence. ("When is your birthday?") Have the students segment *when*.

Encourage the students to pay attention to all the sounds in the word as they write the word on the lined side of their wipe-off boards. Have the students write *when*.

When all the students have finished writing, write *when* on your own wipe-off board. Tell the students that they will check their work by comparing the word they wrote to the one you wrote. Review that when they check, they will compare each letter in the word to make sure all the letters are there and that they are in the same order. Have the students check their work and erase and correct any mistakes they find.

Have the students erase *when*.

Explain that the next word the students will write is a high-frequency word. Say *says*. Use *says* in a sentence. ("Kenji says he likes to read about airplanes.") Ask:

Q *Where can you find the word* says *if you're not sure how to spell it? (on the word wall)*

Have the students write *says*.

When all the students have finished writing, write *says* on your own wipe-off board. Review that the students will check their work by comparing the word they wrote to the one you wrote. Remind them that when they check, they will compare each letter in the word to make sure all the letters are there and that they are in the same order. Have the students check their work and erase and correct any mistakes they find.

Teacher Note

You may wish to point out to the students that two words sound the same but are spelled differently: *which* ("Which book is this?") and *witch* ("A make-believe woman who can do magic".) The students can tell which word is meant by listening to the sentence the word is in. Today's word is *which*, as in "I don't know which book to read first."

Teacher Note

If the students struggle to segment *which*, you might support them by using a visual aid. Draw three blanks side by side on your wipe-off board; then point to each blank in succession as the students say each sound.

To provide more support, you might have the students segment the word, having them write the spelling for each sound as they say it.

Have the students erase *says*. Then collect the wipe-off boards, dry-erase markers, and soft cloths.

Spelling Support

which: Tell the students that in *which* the sound /hw/ is spelled *w-h*, and the sound /ch/ is spelled *c-h*.

when: Tell the students that in *when* the sound /hw/ is spelled *w-h*.

Day 2

Buzz, Hum, Tap, Whap, Whiz, Ding-a-ling
Identifying Middle Sounds;
ng and *-ing; be*

Materials

- Teacher and student copies of *Buzz, Hum, Tap, Whap, Whiz, Ding-a-ling*
- Wipe-off board, dry-erase marker, and tissue or cloth
- Teacher and student bags of sorting pictures, prepared ahead from "Set 3, Week 1 Sort" (BLM1)
- Intact copy of "Set 3, Week 1 Sort" (BLM1), prepared ahead
- High-frequency word card for *be*
- High-frequency word card review deck
- (For Guided Spelling) Wipe-off board, dry-erase marker, and tissue or cloth for each student

Teacher Note

If the students are beginning instruction this week and are learning the procedure for the sound sort (see Step 6), this lesson may require an extended class period.

In this lesson, the students:

- Identify middle sounds
- Learn the spelling-sound *ng* /ng/ and the inflectional ending *-ing* /ing/
- Read decodable words
- Identify beginning sounds
- Learn the procedure for the sound sort
- Learn the high-frequency word *be*
- Review high-frequency words
- Read a new book

1 Gather and Get Ready

Remind the students that during Small-group Reading they will learn new sounds and words, read books, and talk about their reading.

2 Phonological Awareness: Identifying Middle Sounds

Tell the students that today they will listen for the sound they hear in the middle of a word. Explain that you will say a word, and they will say the middle sound. Practice, using the word *pet*. First say the word once normally, then say the word twice, emphasizing the middle sound. Ask:

Q *What sound do you hear in the middle of* pet?

Practice again using a second word, such as *hum*.

If the students struggle to identify the middle sound, you might use a visual aid. Draw three blanks side by side on a wipe-off board. Have the students say the three sounds in *pet* as you point to the blanks. Then point to the middle blank and ask the students to identify the middle sound.

Have the students say the sound they hear in the middle of each of the words that follow. Say the word once normally, then say the word again, emphasizing the middle sound. For each word, ask:

Q *What sound do you hear in the middle of [whip]?*

whip	whiz
job	zap
zip	jet

Teacher Note

If the students are familiar with identifying middle sounds, you do not need to model it here. Instead, simply go to the word list below and remind the students of your expectations for the procedure.

3 Introduce the Spelling-Sound *ng* /ng/ and the Inflectional Ending *-ing* /ing/

Tell the students that today they will learn two spellings that appear frequently in words. Write the spelling *ng* on the lined side of your wipe-off board, point to the spelling, say the letter names, and explain that this spelling stands for the sound /ng/. Have the students repeat the sound as you point to the letters. Then have the students each trace the spelling *n-g* on the table in front of them with one finger as they say /ng/. Write the spelling *i-n-g* on your wipe-off board, point to the spelling, say the letter names, and explain that this spelling stands for the sounds /ing/. Have the students repeat the sounds as you point to the spelling. Then have the students each trace the spelling *i-n-g* on the table in front of them with one finger as they say /ing/.

Explain that the spelling *i-n-g* usually comes at the end of words like *king* or *sing*, and that the spelling *i-n-g* can be added to the end of some words to make new words. Write the pairs *hum/humming* and *tap/tapping* on your wipe-off board and read the words with the students. Use each pair in example sentences, such as "Every day I pat my kitten. Yesterday I was patting my kitten when the doorbell rang."

4 Read Decodable Words

Write the following words on your wipe-off board:

thing	which
song	humming
when	hitting

Point to the left of *thing* and sweep under the word as the students read it. Follow the same procedure for the remaining words on the list.

Teacher Note

You may wish to explain that when we add the ending *-ing* to words such as *hum* that have one short vowel and one consonant at the end, we double the final consonant (except when the consonant is *x*, as in *mixing*).

Decoding Support

If the students struggle to blend decodable words, support them by saying each sound with them while you point to each spelling. Then have the students blend the sounds to read the word. For words with inflectional endings, cover the ending (and any doubled letters) and have the students read the base word in isolation before reading the whole word.

5 Get Ready to Sort: Identifying Beginning Sounds

Explain that the students will learn to listen for the first sound they hear in a word. You will say a word, and then they will say the first sound. Practice, using the word *jog*. Say the word normally; then say the word twice, emphasizing the first sound. Ask:

Q *What sound do you hear at the beginning of* jog?

Segmenting Support

If the students struggle to identify the first sound, you might use a visual aid. Draw three blanks side by side on a wipe-off board and point to each blank as you say the sounds. Then ask the students to say the word slowly as you point to each blank. Finally, point to the first blank and ask the students to identify the first sound.

6 Introduce the Sound Sort

Tell the students that they will sort pictures into two groups. Explain that they will make one group with pictures whose names begin with /j/ and another group with pictures whose names begin with /ch/. Tell them that they will practice sorting pictures now and then sort their pictures during independent word work.

Display the intact "Set 3, Week 1 Sort" sheet (BLM1) and explain that these are the pictures the students will sort this week. Point to each picture and say its name. Then have the students say the names as you point to the pictures.

Take the sorting guide from your own bag of pictures and hold it up. Point out the arrow on the sorting guide (the first square on BLM1). Explain that the arrow pointing to the first blank on the sorting guide means that the students will sort by first sound. Then point to the pictures of the jar and the chair on the sorting guide and explain that these pictures show the sounds the students will match (in this case, /j/ and /ch/).

Tell the students that they will each have their own bag of pictures, and when they begin the sort, they will first find the sorting guide and place it on the table in front of them. Place your sorting guide on the table in front of you. Point to the picture of the jar and say: *jar*, /j/. Then point to the picture of the chair and say: *chair*, /ch/.

Teacher Note

If the students are familiar with identifying beginning sounds, you do not need to model it here. Instead, simply continue to the sound sort in Step 6.

Teacher Note

If the students are familiar with the sound sort, simply display the intact "Set 3, Week 1 Sort" sheet (BLM1) and proceed with the activity.

Teacher Note

Refer to the picture key for this week's sort. See Appendix B, "Sound Sort Picture Key."

Hold up the *cheese* picture from your bag. Ask the students to say the name of the picture and say the beginning sound. Ask:

Q *Does* cheese *begin with /j/? Does* cheese *begin with /ch/? Which picture does* cheese *belong with,* jar *or* chair?

Have a few volunteers share.

Confirm that *cheese* begins with /ch/ and belongs with the *chair* picture. Show the students how to place the *cheese* picture below the *chair* picture. Practice the procedure again, using the *jack-o'-lantern* picture. Hold up the *jack-o'-lantern* picture from your bag. Ask the students to say the name of the picture and then say the beginning sound. Ask:

Q *Does* jack-o'-lantern *begin with /j/? Does* jack-o'-lantern *begin with /ch/? Which picture does the* jack-o'-lantern *belong with,* jar *or* chair?

Confirm that *jack-o'-lantern* begins with /j/ and belongs with *jar*. Place the *jack-o'-lantern* picture below the *jar* picture.

Distribute one bag of sorting pictures to each student. Have the students first find the sorting guide in their bags and place it on the table. Remind them that the arrow pointing to the first blank shows them that they will sort by first sound and that the pictures of the jar and the chair show that they will sort by the sounds /j/ and /ch/.

Ask each student to choose one picture from her bag, say the name of the picture quietly to herself, and decide whether the word starts with /j/ or /ch/. Review that if the word starts with /j/, she will put the picture below the *jar* picture; if the word starts with /ch/, she will put it below the *chair* picture. Support the students as necessary.

When all the students have placed at least one picture, tell them that they will now check their work. Explain that they will say the name of the picture to themselves and listen carefully to what they say. If they have put the picture in the wrong place, they can move it. Practice by checking the pictures you sorted earlier. Point to the *cheese* picture and say: *cheese.* Ask:

Q *Does the word* cheese *start with /ch/? Is the* cheese *picture in the right place?*

Confirm that the *cheese* picture belongs with the *chair* picture because both pictures begin with the sound /ch/. Have each student point to the picture she sorted. Ask each student to say the name of the picture aloud, and think about the first sound in the word. Ask:

Q *Does the name of your picture start with /j/ or /ch/? Is it in the right place?*

Have each student check her picture and move it if necessary. Then have the students check any additional pictures they sorted.

Teacher Note

Depending on how much time you have, you may wish to have the students practice sorting more than one picture each during Small-group Reading.

Explain that when the students go to independent word work, they will sort all their pictures before they do anything else. Briefly review the procedure:

1. Put the sorting guide on the table.

2. Look at another picture and say its name to see if it has the same beginning sound as one of the pictures on the sorting guide: /j/ for *jar* or /ch/ for *chair*.

3. Put all the pictures whose names start with /j/ below the *jar* picture and those that start with /ch/ below the *chair* picture.

4. Check the sort by saying the name of each picture to make sure it is in the right place.

Tell the students that if they need help remembering how to sort their pictures during independent word work, they may quietly ask another student in their reading group to remind them. Have them put their sorting pictures in their bags and put the bags in their toolboxes.

7 Introduce the High-frequency Word *Be*

be   "Will you be here tomorrow?"

Remind the students that *high-frequency words* are words that they will see again and again in their reading. Explain that recognizing these words will help them read stories. Explain that the high-frequency word they will learn today is *be*. Say *be*. Use *be* in a sentence. ("Will you be here tomorrow?") Show the high-frequency word card for *be*, point to the word, and say it as you sweep under it.

Have the students chorally read *be* and then spell *be* as you point to each letter. Then have them read, spell, and read the word again.

If *be* is already on the word wall, point to the word. If it is not, post one word card for *be* on the word wall.

8 Review High-frequency Words

Remind the students that during Small-group Reading lessons they will review some of the words they have learned by reading the words from cards. Explain that when they review a word, they will read it, spell it, and read it again. Show the high-frequency word card for *make*, point to the left of the word, and have the students chorally read it as you sweep under it. Then have the students spell the word as you point under each letter. Finally, have the students read the word as you sweep under it again. Repeat the procedure to review the remaining words in the review deck.

Teacher Note

Add the word card for *be* to the high-frequency word card review deck.

Teacher Note

If you have already taught the procedure for reviewing high-frequency words, simply use it here to review the words you have taught.

Teacher Note

Continue to build the high-frequency word card review deck by adding the cards for the words you introduce to the group.

---

9 Read *Buzz, Hum, Tap, Whap, Whiz, Ding-a-ling*

Distribute a copy of *Buzz, Hum, Tap, Whap, Whiz, Ding-a-ling* to each student. Tell the students that they will read this book today. Show the cover and identify the title and author.

Explain that this book tells about many kinds of sounds we might hear. Open to page 9, and ask the students to find today's new word, *be*. Then ask the students to find the new words *make* and *there* on the same page. Have the students say the words.

Write the words *sound*, *must*, and *something* on your wipe-off board, show the board to the students, and read the words. Have the students say the words. Explain that a sound is something that you hear. Tell the students that they will see these words in today's book. Explain that they will have to remember the words when they see them, or ask you for help. Leave the words on the wipe-off board as a reminder and place the board where everyone can see it.

Explain to the students that when they read their books, they will start on the first page and point to each word on the page as they read it. Tell them that if they finish reading the book, they will turn back to the first page and read it again. Tell the students that they will read out loud today. Point out that all of them will be reading at the same time, so it is important for them to read in quiet voices. Model speaking in a quiet voice. Have all the students turn to page 1 in their own books, point to the first word, and read the first page in quiet voices. If necessary, model again and have the students practice. Have the students read *Buzz, Hum, Tap, Whap, Whiz, Ding-a-ling*.

Monitor the students as they read, and support any student who struggles. When all the students have finished reading, ask:

Q *What are some things that make a humming sound?*

Have a few volunteers share their thinking with the group. Then ask:

Q *What can make a whizzing sound?*

After the students have shared, have them put their books in their toolboxes. Tell them that when they go to independent reading, they will read today's book before reading the other books in their toolboxes.

all read in quiet voices

Teacher Note

If the students are continuing instruction from Set 2, you do not need to repeat the instruction here. Instead, simply have the students read in quiet voices.

Teacher Note

If your group is continuing, see "Spelling Support" below.

Teacher Note

If the students struggle to segment *whiz*, you might support them with a visual aid. Draw three blanks side by side on your wipe-off board. Point to each blank in succession as the students say each sound.

Teacher Note

If the students have trouble checking their work, model the procedure as you did on Day 1.

Teacher Note

It is not possible to segment words with /ng/ or /ing/ or with inflectional endings in a way that supports spelling. If necessary, support the students by asking them more generally to listen for all the sounds in a word before they write it.

GUIDED SPELLING

whiz	"I heard something whiz by me."
thing	"What is your favorite thing to draw?"
so	"I am so happy to be here."

Distribute wipe-off boards, dry-erase markers, and tissues or pieces of soft cloth to the students.

Say *whiz*. Use *whiz* in a sentence. ("I heard something whiz by me.") Have the students segment *whiz*.

Have the students write *whiz*.

When all the students have finished writing, write *whiz* on your own wipe-off board. Have the students check their work and erase and correct any mistakes they find.

Have the students erase *whiz*.

Say *thing*. Use *thing* in a sentence. ("What is your favorite thing to draw?") Have the students write *thing*.

When all the students have finished writing, write *thing* on your own wipe-off board. Have the students check their work and erase and correct any mistakes they find.

Have the students erase *thing*.

Explain that the next word the students will write is a high-frequency word. Say *so*. Use *so* in a sentence. ("I am so happy to be here.") Ask:

Q *Where can you find the word* so *if you're not sure how to spell it? (on the word wall)*

Have the students write *so*.

When all the students have finished writing, write *so* on your own wipe-off board. Have the students check their work and erase and correct any mistakes they find.

Have the students erase *so*. Then collect the wipe-off boards, dry-erase markers, and soft cloths.

Spelling Support

whiz: Tell the students that in *whiz* the sound /hw/ is spelled *w-h*.

Buzz, Hum, Tap, Whap, Whiz, Ding-a-ling
Blending Onsets and Rimes; Review and Reread

In this lesson, the students:

- Blend onsets and rimes
- Review spelling-sounds
- Review high-frequency words
- Read a familiar book

ABOUT THE INDIVIDUAL READING OBSERVATION

This week you will begin the Individual Reading Observation (IR). This assessment, conducted every other week, gives you the opportunity to listen to individual students and make notes about their reading accuracy and automaticity. While mastery tests tell you whether a student has mastered the phonics and high-frequency word content, this more frequent and informal assessment of each student's reading provides other important information. By recording your observations about a particular student over time, you will develop a clear sense of her strengths and weaknesses as a reader. For more information, see "Individual Reading Observation" in the Assessment Overview of the *Assessment Resource Book*.

1 Gather and Get Ready

Explain that today the students will review sounds and words they have already learned and read their small-group books again.

2 Phonological Awareness: Blending Onsets and Rimes

Tell the students that they will put sounds together to make words. Explain that you will say a word in two parts; then they will put the parts together to make a word. Model the procedure, using the word *fed*. Say the sounds slowly and clearly three times, isolating the beginning sound (onset) from the rest of the word (rime): /ff/ . . . ed. Then say the sounds more quickly, blending them to say the word. Say the sounds again: /ff/ . . . ed. Have the students repeat the sounds, /f/ . . . ed, and then blend them to say the word. If necessary, practice using a second word, such as *red*.

Materials

- Teacher and student copies of *Buzz, Hum, Tap, Whap, Whiz, Ding-a-ling* from Day 2
- Sound card review deck
- High-frequency word card review deck
- Wipe-off board, dry-erase marker, and tissue or cloth
- Group set of the "Individual Reading Observation" sheet (IR1), prepared ahead
- (For Guided Spelling) Wipe-off board, dry-erase marker, and tissue or cloth for each student

Blending Support

If the students have difficulty blending, you might use a visual aid. Draw a blank and a box side by side on a wipe-off board. Point to the blank as you say the onset and the box as you say the rime. Sweep under the blank and box as you say the word. Then have the students say the sounds as you point to the blank and box and say the word as you sweep under them. You might also point out that only the first sound changes from word to word.

Have the students blend each of the following words after you say the onset and rime:

/f/ . . . **ed**	fed
/r/ . . . **ed**	red
/t/ . . . **ed**	Ted
/n/ . . . **ed**	Ned
/w/ . . . **ed**	wed
/l/ . . . **ed**	led

3 Review Spelling-Sounds

Tell the students that they will use cards to review the sounds they are learning. Explain that they will say the sound of the spelling when they see it. Model by displaying the sound card for *wh*, pointing to the spelling, and saying /hw/. Have the students say /hw/ as you point to the spelling. Then display the sound card for *wh* and have the students say the sound /hw/.

4 Review High-frequency Words

Remind the students that when they review words they have learned, they will read each word, spell it, and read it again. Show the high-frequency word card for *some*, point to the left of the word, and have the students chorally read it as you sweep under it. Then have the students spell the word as you point under each letter. Finally, have the students read the word as you sweep under it again. Use the same procedure to review the remaining words in the review deck.

5 Reread *Buzz, Hum, Tap, Whap, Whiz, Ding-a-ling*

Have the students take *Buzz, Hum, Tap, Whap, Whiz, Ding-a-ling* from their toolboxes. Read the title aloud with the students. Write the words *sound*, *must*, and *something* on your wipe-off board and say the words. Remind the students that they will see these words in the book and they will have to remember the words when they see them, or ask you for help. Then explain that today the students will read the book in quiet voices. Remind the students that if they finish reading, they will go back to the first page and read the book again. Have the students read *Buzz, Hum, Tap, Whap, Whiz, Ding-a-ling*.

Teacher Note

Build the review deck by adding the sound cards for the sounds you introduce to the group. After you have accumulated about 20 cards, begin removing cards for sounds the students know well.

Teacher Note

Continue to build the review deck by adding the word cards for the words you introduce to the group. After you have accumulated about 20 cards, begin removing cards for words the students know well.

☑ **INDIVIDUAL READING OBSERVATION NOTE**

Listen to a few students as they read, taking notes on the "Individual Reading Observation" sheet (IR1) and offering support as needed; see page 144 of the *Assessment Resource Book*.

6 Check Comprehension and Reflect

When all the students have finished reading, ask and briefly discuss:

Q *Which are loud sounds? Which are soft sounds?*

Q *What are some sounds we can hear in the classroom right now?*

Have students return their books to their toolboxes. Remind them that when they go to independent reading, they will read today's book before reading the other books in their toolboxes.

GUIDED SPELLING

She can sing.

Distribute wipe-off boards, dry-erase markers, and tissues or pieces of soft cloth to the students. Explain that today the students will write a sentence.

Say: *She can sing.* Have the students repeat the sentence. Then ask:

Q *What's the first word? (She)*

Q *Where will you find the word* she *if you are not sure how to spell it? (on the word wall)*

Q *What's special about the first word in a sentence? (It has a capital letter.)*

Have the students write *She*. Then ask:

Q *What's the next word? (can)*

Have the students write *can*. Then ask:

Q *What's the next word? (sing)*

Have the students write *sing*. Then ask:

Q *What mark do we need at the end of a sentence? (a period)*

When all the students have finished writing, write the sentence on your own wipe-off board. Have the students check their work and erase and correct any mistakes they find.

Have the students erase the sentence. Then collect the wipe-off boards, dry-erase markers, and soft cloths.

Teacher Note

If your group is continuing, simply support the students in writing the sentence as you did in previous lessons.

Teacher Note

If necessary, support the students by asking them to identify whether each word in the sentence is a high-frequency word or one that they can sound out.

Teacher Note

If the students have trouble keeping track of the sentence, you might support them with a visual aid. Draw three boxes side by side on your wipe-off board. Point to each in succession as the students say the sentence.

Teacher Note

If necessary, tell the students that every sentence ends with a punctuation mark. This sentence ends with a period.

RESOURCES

New	Revisit	Practice or Reteach

The Good Little Ducks, Part 1

by Corinn Kintz, illustrated by Barbara Gibson

Buzz, Hum, Tap, Whap, Whiz, Ding-a-ling

by Corinn Kintz

The Good Little Ducks, Part 2

by Corinn Kintz, illustrated by Barbara Gibson

Reteaching
- "Reteach with *The Good Little Ducks, Part 2*"

Assessment Resource Book
- Week 2 assessment

Sound Cards
- _ed /t/, /d/, /əd/
- qu /khw/

High-frequency Word Cards
- *look*
- *good*

Wipe-off Boards

 Online Resources

Visit the CCC Learning Hub (ccclearninghub.org) to find your online resources for this week.

Assessment Form
- "Group Progress Assessment" sheet (GA1)

Reproducible
- "Set 3, Week 2 Sort" (BLM2)

OVERVIEW

Spelling-Sound Focus
- inflectional ending -ed /t/, /d/, /əd/
- qu /khw/ (queen)

High-frequency Words
- look
- good

⏱ DO AHEAD

✓ Prior to Day 1, add high-frequency word cards for *look* and *good* to the word wall if they are not already displayed.

✓ Prior to Day 2, visit the CCC Learning Hub (ccclearninghub.org) to access and print "Set 3, Week 2 Sort" (BLM2). Make a copy for each student in the group, plus two. Cut apart the pictures on each sheet (keeping one copy intact) to create a set of sorting pictures for ending sounds /d/ and /t/ for each student in the group and one for yourself. Place each set of cards in a resealable plastic bag.

✓ Prior to Day 3, add the sound cards for _ed and qu to the sound card review deck.

✓ Prior to Day 3, make a copy of the "Group Progress Assessment" sheet (GA1); see page 168 of the *Assessment Resource Book*.

🌐 ELL SUPPORT

- **-ed**

  In Spanish, the final consonant *d* stands for a soft sound similar to /th/. When you introduce -ed, point out the difference in English. Model producing /d/ with the tongue placed on the bony plate behind the top teeth and a voiced burst of air. When you introduce the three sounds of -ed, model each pronunciation and provide several example words for each.

- **qu**

  There is no equivalent for the combined sounds /khw/ in Spanish, Chinese dialects, or Hmong. Model producing the separate sounds /k/ and /hw/. Then have students blend the sounds to say /khw/. To hear the recommended pronunciation for the spelling *qu*, view the Pronunciation Guide video on the CCC Learning Hub.

(continues)

🌐 ELL SUPPORT   *(continued)*

- **qu**

  In Spanish, the spelling *qu* stands for the /k/ sound before the letters *i* or *e*. Spanish-speaking students may omit the /hw/ sound when blending English words with *qu*. For example, these students may say *kit* for *quit*. To help them produce /khw/, explain that it is like the sounds they hear in the middle of the Spanish word *escuela* (ehs-KWAY-lah), "school."

Buzz, Hum, Tap, Whap, Whiz, Ding-a-ling

Oral Blending;
Inflectional Ending -ed and *look*

In this lesson, the students:

- Practice oral blending
- Learn the inflectional ending *-ed* /t/, /d/, /əd/
- Read decodable words
- Learn the high-frequency word *look*
- Review high-frequency words
- Read a familiar book

Materials

- Teacher and student copies of *Buzz, Hum, Tap, Whap, Whiz, Ding-a-ling* from Week 1
- Wipe-off board, dry-erase marker, and tissue or cloth
- High-frequency word card for *look*
- High-frequency word card review deck

1 Phonological Awareness: Oral Blending

Have the students blend each of the words that follow after you say the phonemes, using continuous blending. Clap softly as you say each sound. Then brush your hands past each other as the students say the word.

/tĕĕd/	Ted
/păăd/	pad
/jŏŏt/	jot
/zzăăp/	zap
/llĕĕt/	let
/rrĕĕd/	red

2 Introduce the Inflectional Ending *-ed* /t/, /d/, /əd/

Tell the students that today they will learn the word ending *e-d*. Explain that when *e-d* is added to an action word, it shows that the action happened in the past. Write the following pairs of words on your wipe-off board:

drop/dropped   lift/lifted

tag/tagged

Read the word pairs to the students. Ask:

Q *What do you notice about these words?*

> **Students might say:**
>
> "They all end with the letters *e-d*."
>
> "They have different sounds at the end."

ELL Note

English Language Learners may not have the vocabulary knowledge to know which pronunciation "sounds right." You may have to model the correct pronunciation and have the students repeat what you say.

Decoding Support

Reading words with inflectional endings is challenging. You may wish to support the students by covering the ending (including any doubled consonant) and having the students read the base word alone. Then uncover the ending and have them read the entire word. Another option is to write just the base word, have the students read that, double the final consonant if needed, add the ending, and have the students read the inflected word.

Teacher Note

Add the word card for *look* to the high-frequency word card review deck.

Tell the students that the ending *e-d* can stand for three different sounds. Sometimes the sound is /t/, as in *dropped*; sometimes it is /d/, as in *tagged*; and sometimes it is /əd/, as in *lifted*. Point out that when *e-d* is added to the words *drop* and *tag*, the last letter in the word is doubled.

Have the students read each pair of words with you as you point to them. Tell the students that when they see *e-d* at the end of a word, they will have to say the word to hear which sound—/t/, /d/, or /əd/—sounds right.

3 Read Decodable Words

Write the following words on your wipe-off board:

tipped	checked
ducked	nodded
hopping	batted

Point to each word and sweep under it as the students read it.

4 Introduce the High-frequency Word *Look*

> look   "Look at the colorful rainbow."

Introduce *look* by saying the word as you show the word card to the students. Use the word in a sentence. Have the students read it and spell it twice, and then read it a third time.

5 Review High-frequency Words

Review the previously introduced high-frequency words by showing each word in the review deck and having the students read it, spell it, and read it again.

6 Reread *Buzz, Hum, Tap, Whap, Whiz, Ding-a-ling*

Have the students take the book *Buzz, Hum, Tap, Whap, Whiz, Ding-a-ling* from their toolboxes. Tell the students that they will reread this book today. Read the title with the students and ask:

Q *What are some of the things in this book that make noise?*

Have a few volunteers share their thinking with the group. Then have the students read the book in quiet voices.

Monitor the students as they read, and support any student who struggles. When all the students have finished reading, collect the books or have the students return their books to their toolboxes.

GUIDED SPELLING

back	"Our fish tank is in the back of the classroom."
wing	"The bird's wing was hurt."
make	"Will you make me a sandwich?"

Guide the students through spelling each of the decodable words, paying particular attention to sounds that can be spelled in more than one way. Then have them write the high-frequency word. Refer to Week 1, Day 1 Guided Spelling for the detailed procedure.

Spelling Support

back: Remind the students that the sound /k/ at the end of a word is usually spelled *c-k*. Tell the students that in *back* the sound /k/ is spelled *c-k*.

The Good Little Ducks, Part 1
Identifying Middle Sounds; *qu* and *good*

Day 2

In this lesson, the students:

- Identify middle sounds
- Learn the spelling-sound *qu* /khw/
- Read decodable words
- Identify last sounds for the sound sort
- Learn the high-frequency word *good*
- Review high-frequency words
- Read a new book

Materials

- Teacher and student copies of *The Good Little Ducks, Part 1*
- Wipe-off board, dry-erase marker, and tissue or cloth
- Teacher and student bags of sorting pictures, prepared ahead from "Set 3, Week 2 Sort" (BLM2)
- Intact copy of "Set 3, Week 2 Sort" (BLM2), prepared ahead
- High-frequency word card for *good*
- High-frequency word card review deck

1 Phonological Awareness: Identifying Middle Sounds

Have the students say the sound they hear in the middle of each of the following words:

match	fetch
chin	chop
zip	jet

2 Introduce the Spelling-Sound *qu* /khw/

Explain that today's sound is /khw/, and have the students say the sound. Point to the alphabet wall card for *Qq.* Explain that the picture of the queen will help them remember the sound /khw/ because the word *queen* begins with the sound /khw/. Write *qu* on your wipe-off board, point to the spelling, and say the letter names. Tell the students that the spelling *q-u* stands for the sound /khw/. Have the students repeat the sound as you point to the spelling. Then have the students each trace the spelling *q-u* on the table in front of them with one finger as they say /khw/.

3 Read Decodable Words

Write the following words on your wipe-off board:

quack	quick
nodded	running
quit	latch

Point to each word and sweep under it as the students read it. For *latch,* explain that a latch is a type of door lock.

4 Introduce the Sound Sort

Ask and briefly discuss:

Q *How did you do with sorting last week? What questions do you have about sorting?*

Explain that this week, the students will sort pictures by last sound. Display the intact "Set 3, Week 2 Sort" sheet (BLM2) and explain that these are the pictures the students will sort this week. Point to each picture and say its name. Then have the students say the names as you point to the pictures.

Take the sorting guide from your own bag of pictures and hold it up. Point out the arrow on the sorting guide (the first square on BLM2). Explain that the arrow pointing to the last blank on the sorting guide means that the students will sort by last sound. Then point to the pictures of the bed and the cat on the sorting guide. Explain that these pictures show the sounds the students will match (in this case, /d/ and /t/).

Place your sorting guide on the table in front of you. Point to the picture of the bed and say: *bed,* /d/. Then point to the picture of the cat and say: *cat,* /t/. Hold up the *bat* picture from your bag. Ask:

Q *What sound do you hear at the end of* bat?

Confirm that *bat* ends with the sound /t/ and model placing the picture below the *cat* picture. Practice the procedure again, using the *hand* picture.

Distribute one bag of sorting pictures to each student. Have the students first find the sorting guide and place it on the table. Remind them that the arrow pointing to the last blank will remind them to sort by last sound. Review that the pictures of the bed and the cat show that they will sort by the last sounds /d/ and /t/.

Ask each student to choose one picture from his bag, say the name of the picture quietly to himself, and decide whether the word ends with /d/ or /t/. Review that if the word ends with /d/, he will put the picture below the *bed* picture; if it ends with /t/, he will put it below the *cat* picture. Support the students as necessary.

When all the students have placed at least one picture, tell them that they will now check their work. Explain that they will say the name of the picture to themselves and listen carefully to what they say. If they have put a picture in the wrong place, they can move it. Model by checking the *hand* picture. Point to the *hand* picture and say: *hand.* Ask:

Q *Does the word* hand *end with /d/? Is the* hand *picture in the right place?*

Have each student check his picture and move it if necessary. Then have the students check any additional pictures they sorted.

Tell the students that if they need help remembering how to sort their pictures during independent word work, they may quietly ask another student in their reading group to remind them. Have them put their sorting pictures in their bags and put the bags in their toolboxes.

5 Introduce the High-frequency Word *Good*

good   "Eating fruit is good for us."

Introduce *good* by saying the word as you show the word card to the students. Use the word in a sentence. Have the students read it and spell it twice, and then read it a third time.

6 Review High-frequency Words

Review the previously introduced high-frequency words by showing each word in the review deck and having the students read it, spell it, and read it again.

7 Read *The Good Little Ducks, Part 1*

Distribute a copy of *The Good Little Ducks, Part 1* to each student. Tell the students that they will read this book today. Read the title with the students and identify the names of the author and illustrator. Tell the students that this story is about three little ducks. Open to page 1, and ask the students to find today's new word *good.* Then turn to page 2, and ask the students to find the new word *look.*

Teacher Note

Add the word card for *good* to the high-frequency word card review deck.

Teacher Note

Consonant blends are formally introduced beginning in Week 3. For this week, support the students in reading the words with blends that appear in *The Good Little Ducks*.

Teacher Note

You may wish to point out to the students that three words sound the same: *there* (as in "over there"), *their* (meaning "belonging to them"), and *they're* (an abbreviation for "they are"). The students can tell which word it is by listening to the sentence the word is in. Today's word is *there*, as in "The books are there in the library."

Write the words *pond, swim*, and *jump* on your wipe-off board and tell the students that they will see these words in their reading today. Have them sound out each word and then read it. If necessary, read the words for the students. Add *-ed* to *jump* and read the word *jumped* for the students. Have the students say the word.

Write *watch* on your wipe-off board and read it for the students. Have the students say the word. Tell the students that they will see this word in today's story. Explain that they will have to remember this word when they see it, or ask you for help. Leave the word on the wipe-off board as a reminder and place the board where everyone can see it. Have the students turn to page 1 in their books and read the story in quiet voices.

Monitor the students as they read, and support any student who struggles. When all the students have finished reading, ask:

Q *What do the little ducks do in this story?*

Q *How do the pictures help you understand the story?*

Have the students put their books in their toolboxes. Remind the students that when they go to independent reading, they will read today's book before reading the other books in their toolboxes.

GUIDED SPELLING

thing	"A jackhammer is a thing that makes a loud noise."
quit	"We all quit playing the game."
there	"I see a tree over there."

Guide the students through spelling each of the decodable words, paying particular attention to sounds that can be spelled in more than one way. Then have them write the high-frequency word. Refer to Week 1, Day 1 Guided Spelling for the detailed procedure.

Spelling Support

quit: Tell the students that in *quit* the sound /khw/ is spelled *q-u*.

The Good Little Ducks, Part 1
Blending Onsets and Rimes; Review and Reread

Day 3

In this lesson, the students:

- Blend onsets and rimes
- Review spelling-sounds
- Review high-frequency words
- Read a familiar book

1 Phonological Awareness: Blending Onsets and Rimes

Have the students blend each of the following onsets and rimes after you say the phonemes:

/p/ . . . ill	pill
/f/ . . . ill	fill
/b/ . . . ill	bill
/h/ . . . ill	hill
/khw/ . . . ill	quill
/w/ . . . ill	will

2 Review Spelling-Sounds

Use the sound card review deck to have the students say the sound of each spelling.

3 Review High-frequency Words

Review the previously introduced high-frequency words by showing each word in the review deck and having the students read it, spell it, and read it again.

4 Reread *The Good Little Ducks, Part 1*

Have the students take *The Good Little Ducks, Part 1* from their toolboxes and tell them that they will reread this story today. Read the title aloud with the students. Write the words *jumped* and *watch* on your wipe-off board, say the words, and remind the students that they will see these words in today's book. Remind them that they will have to remember the words when they see them, or ask for help. Leave the words on the wipe-off board as a reminder and place the board where everyone can see it.

Materials

- Teacher and students copies of *The Good Little Ducks, Part 1* from Day 2
- Sound card review deck
- High-frequency word card review deck
- Wipe-off board, dry-erase marker, and tissue or cloth
- "Group Progress Assessment" sheet (GA1)

Teacher Note

When you review the sound card for _ed, always have the students say the sounds in the same order: /t/, /d/, /əd/.

Remind the students that if they finish reading, they will go back to the first page and read the book again. Have the students read *The Good Little Ducks, Part 1* in quiet voices.

GROUP PROGRESS ASSESSMENT NOTE

As you observe the group, ask yourself:

- Do the students look at the illustrations to confirm that what they read makes sense?
- Can the students read words with inflectional endings?

Record your observations on the "Group Progress Assessment" sheet (GA1); see page 168 of the *Assessment Resource Book*. Support struggling students by reteaching previous content; see "Reteach with *The Good Little Ducks, Part 2*" on the next page. If the students struggle with inflectional endings, provide additional practice. Create several lists of five or six CVC words with inflectional endings and have students read one or more of the lists until they have mastered them.

Teacher Note

You may wish to have students who do not require reteaching put *The Good Little Ducks, Part 2* in their toolboxes for independent reading. If so, introduce the words *something*, *pond*, and *jumped* by writing them on your wipe-off board, saying the words, and explaining that the students will see these words in the book.

Teacher Note

If the students do not mention it, explain that the pictures in a book can help readers understand a story. For example, you might show the illustration on page 12, read the text aloud, and ask, "What do you see in the illustration that helps you know how the ducks feel?"

5 Check Comprehension and Reflect

When all the students have finished reading, ask and briefly discuss:

Q *What do the ducks do in the pond?*

Q *How do the little ducks feel about the pond? How do you know?*

Have the students return their books to their toolboxes. Remind them that when they go to independent reading, they will read today's book before reading the other books in their toolboxes.

GUIDED SPELLING

The ducks quacked.

Guide the students through the sentence, word by word. Refer to Week 1, Day 3 Guided Spelling for the detailed procedure.

Spelling Support

ducks: Support the students in writing the base word, *duck*. Remind the students that the sound /k/ at the end of a word is usually spelled *c-k*. Tell the students that in *duck* the sound /k/ is spelled *c-k*. Support the students in adding the inflectional ending to write *ducks*.

quacked: Support the students in writing the base word, *quack*. Tell the students that in *quack* the sound /khw/ is spelled *q-u*. Remind the students that the sound /k/ at the end of a word is usually spelled *c-k*. Tell the students that in *quack* the sound /k/ is spelled *c-k*. Then support the students in adding the inflectional ending to write *quacked*.

RETEACHING

Reteach with *The Good Little Ducks, Part 2*

Review the spelling-sounds *wh* /hw/; *ng* /ng/, *-ing* /ing/; *-ed* /d/, /t/, /əd/; and *qu* /khw/; and the high-frequency words *make, there, be, look,* and *good.* Use the book *The Good Little Ducks, Part 2* for reading practice.

After reading the title aloud with the students, write the word *something* on your wipe-off board, and explain that this word is made up of two smaller words. Cover *thing* and have the students read *some.* Then cover *some* and have the students read *thing.* Then have them read the whole word. Tell the students that they will have to remember the word *something* when they see it, or ask for help. Leave the word on your wipe-off board as a reminder and place the board where everyone can see it. If necessary, review *pond* and *jumped* as you did on Day 2, Step 7.

Explain that the students will read the book in quiet voices. Review that students who finish reading will go back to the first page and read the book again. Have the students read *The Good Little Ducks, Part 2.*

When all the students have finished reading, ask and briefly discuss:

Q *What happens in this story?*

Q *How does the mother duck feel? How can you tell?*

Collect the books or have the students put their books in their toolboxes.

Teacher Note

If you have students who are struggling to learn the sounds and words you have taught in the previous two weeks, you might provide an additional week of instruction before introducing new sounds and words. For more information, see "Reteaching" in the Introduction.

Inflectional endings are particularly difficult for students. You may wish to reteach this week with the whole group to solidify their learning.

RESOURCES

New

The Jug of Water

by Rob Arego,
illustrated by Adam Record

Revisit

***The Good Little
Ducks, Part 1***

by Corinn Kintz,
illustrated by
Barbara Gibson

Assessment Resource Book

- Week 3 assessment

Sound Cards

- *sn* /sn/
- *st* /st/

High-frequency Word Cards

- *want*
- *water*
- *from*

Wipe-off Boards

 Online Resources

Visit the CCC Learning Hub (ccclearninghub.org) to find your online resources for this week.

Assessment Form

- "Individual Reading Observation" sheet (IR1)

Reproducible

- "Set 3, Week 3 Sort" (BLM3)

OVERVIEW

Spelling-Sound Focus	High-frequency Words
• *sn* /sn/	• *want*
• *st* /st/	• *water*
	• *from*

⏱ DO AHEAD

✓ Prior to Day 1, add high-frequency word cards for *want, water,* and *from* to the word wall if they are not already displayed.

✓ Prior to Day 2, visit the CCC learning Hub (ccclearninghub.org) to access and print "Set 3, Week 3 Sort" (BLM3). Make a copy for each student in the group, plus two. Cut apart the pictures on each sheet (keeping one copy intact) to create a set of sorting pictures for middle sound /ă/ and middle sound /ĕ/ for each student in the group and one for yourself. Place each set of pictures in a resealable plastic bag.

✓ Prior to Day 3, add the sound cards for *sn* and *st* to the sound card review deck.

🌐 ELL SUPPORT

• **sn, st**

There are no initial or final *s* consonant blends in Spanish. The spellings *sn* and *st* only occur in separate syllables, such as in *cisne* (SEEZ-nay), "swan," and *estar* (ay-STAHR), "to be." The students may add a vowel sound before the initial consonant and after the final consonant in words with *s* consonant blends.

• **sn, st**

There are no initial consonant clusters in Chinese. The students may insert a slight vowel sound between the consonants.

• **water**

If you created a mnemonic display in Week 1, add the word *water* next to the *r*-controlled *her* (bird mnemonic).

Day 1

The Good Little Ducks, Part 1
Oral Blending;
sn; *want* and *water*

Materials

- Teacher and student copies of *The Good Little Ducks, Part 1* from Week 2
- Wipe-off board, dry-erase marker, and tissue or cloth
- High-frequency word card for *want*
- High-frequency word card for *water*
- High-frequency word card review deck

Decoding Support

When saying sounds, try to say the pure sounds (/sssnnn/) without adding a slight vowel (/sssnnnŭ/).

🌐 ELL Note

You may wish to have the students practice saying additional words beginning with *sn*, such as **sn**ow, **sn**ap, and **sn**ip.

In this lesson, the students:

- Practice oral blending
- Learn the consonant blend *sn* /sn/
- Read decodable words
- Learn the high-frequency words *want* and *water*
- Review high-frequency words
- Read a familiar book

1 Phonological Awareness: Oral Blending

Have the students blend each of the words that follow after you say the phonemes, using continuous blending. Clap softly as you say each sound. Then brush your hands past each other as the students say the word.

/ssnnĭĭff/	sniff
/ssnnăăp/	snap
/ssnnĭĭp/	snip
/ssnnăăg/	snag
/ssnnŭŭg/	snug
/ssnnăăk/	snack

2 Introduce the Consonant Blend *sn* /sn/

Explain that today the students will learn a pair of letters that they will often see together at the beginning of words. Write the spelling *sn* on your wipe-off board. Explain that when the students see the letters *s* and *n* together, they will blend the sounds. Point to the left of *sn* and sweep under the spelling as you say /sn/. Have the students blend the sounds as you sweep under the spelling. Then say each of the words that follow, emphasizing the beginning blend. Have the students repeat each word: *snake, sneeze, snack*.

Have the students each trace the spelling *sn* on the table in front of them with one finger as they say /sn/.

3 Read Decodable Words

Write the following words on your wipe-off board:

snapped	jug
snack	song
ringing	help

Point to each word and sweep under it as the students read it.

4 Introduce the High-frequency Words *Want* and *Water*

want   "I want to be a painter."

Introduce *want* by saying the word as you show the word card to the students. Use the word in a sentence. Have the students read it and spell it twice, and then read it a third time.

5 Review High-frequency Words

Review the previously introduced high-frequency words by showing each word in the review deck and having the students read it, spell it, and read it again.

6 Reread *The Good Little Ducks, Part 1*

Have the students take the book *The Good Little Ducks, Part 1* from their toolboxes. Tell the students that they will reread this book today. Read the title with the students and ask:

Q *What do the little ducks in this story do?*

Have a few volunteers share their thinking with the group. Then have the students read the book in quiet voices.

Monitor the students as they read, and support any student who struggles. When all the students have finished reading, collect the books or have the students return their books to their toolboxes.

Decoding Support

Support struggling students by covering the ending and having the students read the base word alone. Then uncover the ending and have them read the entire word. Another option is to write just the base word, have the students read that, add the ending, and have the students read the inflected word.

Teacher Note

Add the word cards for *want* and *water* to the high-frequency word card review deck.

GUIDED SPELLING

snap	"I can snap my fingers."
king	"Some countries have a king and a queen."
look	"It's fun to look at clouds."

Spelling Support

king: Tell the students that in *king* the sound /k/ is spelled *k*.

Guide the students through spelling each of the decodable words, paying particular attention to sounds that can be spelled in more than one way. Then have them write the high-frequency word.

Day 2

The Jug of Water
Oral Segmenting;
st and *from*

Materials

- Teacher and student copies of *The Jug of Water*
- Wipe-off board, dry-erase marker, and tissue or cloth
- Teacher and student bags of sorting pictures, prepared ahead from "Set 3, Week 3 Sort" (BLM3)
- Intact copy of "Set 3, Week 3 Sort" (BLM3), prepared ahead
- High-frequency word card for *from*
- High-frequency word card review deck

In this lesson, the students:

- Practice oral segmenting
- Learn the consonant blend *st* /st/
- Read decodable words
- Identify middle sounds for the sound sort
- Learn the high-frequency word *from*
- Review high-frequency words
- Read a new book

1 Phonological Awareness: Oral Segmenting

Have the students segment the phonemes after you say each of the words that follow. Have them clap softly as they say each sound. Then for each word, ask:

Q *How many sounds are in the word [mist]?*

mist	/m/ /ĭ/ /s/ /t/
stiff	/s/ /t/ /ĭ/ /f/
step	/s/ /t/ /ĕ/ /p/
stuck	/s/ /t/ /ŭ/ /k/
past	/p/ /ă/ /s/ /t/
stack	/s/ /t/ /ă/ /k/

2 Introduce the Consonant Blend *st* /st/

Explain that today the students will learn a pair of letters that they will often see together at the beginning of words. Write the spelling *st* on your wipe-off board. Explain that when the students see the letters *s* and *t* together, they will blend the sounds. Point to the left of *st* and sweep under the spelling as you say /st/. Have the students blend the sounds as you sweep under the spelling. Then say each of the words that follow, emphasizing the beginning blend. Have the students repeat each word: *stiff, stamp, stack.*

 ELL Note

You may wish to have the students practice saying additional words beginning with *st*, such as ***st**ick,* ***st**ep,* and ***st**ar.*

Tell the students that they will also see *s* and *t* together at the end of words. Say each of the words that follow, emphasizing the ending blend. Have the students repeat each word: *last, best, list.*

Have the students each trace the spelling *st* on the table in front of them with one finger as they say /st/.

3 Read Decodable Words

Write the following words on your wipe-off board:

Stan	stuck
snap	still
snuck	padded

Point to each word and sweep under it as the students read it.

Decoding Support

Support struggling students by covering the ending (including any doubled consonant) and having the students read the base word alone. Then uncover the ending and have them read the entire word. Another option is to write just the base word, have the students read that, double the final consonant if needed, add the ending, and have the students read the inflected word.

4 Introduce the Sound Sort

Remind the students that they have been sorting pictures by first sound and last sound. Tell the students that this week they will sort pictures by middle sound. Display the intact "Set 3, Week 3 Sort" sheet (BLM3) and explain that these are the pictures the students will sort this week. Point to each picture, and say its name. Then have the students say the names as you point to the pictures.

Take the sorting guide from your own bag of pictures and hold it up. Point out the arrow on the sorting guide (the first square on BLM3). Explain that the arrow pointing to the middle blank on the sorting guide means that the students will sort by middle sound. Then point to the pictures of the cat and the net on the sorting guide and explain that these pictures show the middle sounds the students will match (in this case, /ă/ and /ĕ/).

Place your sorting guide on the table in front of you. Point to the picture of the cat and say: *cat,* /ă/. Then point to the picture of the net and say: *net,* /ĕ/. Hold up the *web* picture from your bag. Ask:

Q *What sound do you hear in the middle of* web?

Confirm that *web* has the middle sound /ĕ/ and model placing the picture below the *net* picture. Practice the procedure again, using the *fan* picture. Distribute one bag of pictures to each student. Have the students first find the sorting guide and place it on the table. Remind them that the arrow pointing to the middle blank will remind them to sort by middle sound. Review that the pictures of the cat and the net show that they will sort by the middle sounds /ă/ and /ĕ/.

Ask each student to choose one picture from her bag, say the name of the picture quietly to herself, and decide whether the word has the middle sound /ă/ or /ĕ/. Review that if the word has the middle sound /ă/, she will put the picture below the *cat* picture; if it has the middle sound /ĕ/, she will put it below the *net* picture. Support the students as necessary.

Teacher Note

Refer to the picture key for this week's sort. See Appendix B, "Sound Sort Picture Key."

Teacher Note

If necessary, support the students in identifying middle sound by repeating the question for other pictures on the sheet of sorting pictures.

When all the students have placed at least one picture, tell them that they will now check their work. Explain that they will say the name of the picture to themselves and listen carefully to what they say. If they have put a picture in the wrong place, they can move it. Model by checking the *fan* picture. Point to the *fan* picture and say: *fan*. Ask:

Q *Does the word* fan *have the middle sound /ă/? Is the* fan *picture in the right place?*

Have each student check her picture and move it if necessary. Then have the students check any additional pictures they sorted.

Tell the students that if they need help remembering how to sort their pictures during independent word work, they may quietly ask another student in their reading group to remind them. Have them put their sorting pictures in their bags and put the bags in their toolboxes.

5 Introduce the High-frequency Word *from*

from   "My family came here from Mexico."

Introduce *from* by saying the word as you show the word card to the students. Use the word in a sentence. Have the students read it and spell it twice, and then read it a third time.

6 Review High-frequency Words

Review the previously introduced high-frequency words by showing each word in the review deck and having the students read it, spell it, and read it again.

7 Read *The Jug of Water*

Distribute a copy of *The Jug of Water* to each student. Tell the students that they will read this book today. Read the title with the students and identify the names of the author and illustrator. Tell the students that this story is about some animals that get stuck in a house. Open to page 3, and ask the students to find today's new word, *from*. Ask them to find the new word *water* on the same page. Then turn to page 6 and ask the students to find the new word *want*.

Write the word *wanted* on your wipe-off board and tell the students that they will see the word in their reading today. Cover the inflectional ending and have the students read the high-frequency word *want*. Then uncover the inflectional ending and have them read the whole word.

Write the word *more* on your wipe-off board and read it for the students. Have the students say the word. Tell the students that they will see this word in today's story. Explain that they will have to remember the word when they see it, or ask you for help. Leave the word on the wipe-off board as a reminder and place the board where everyone can see it. Have the students turn to page 1 in their books and read the story in quiet voices.

🌐 ELL Note

English Language Learners may benefit from hearing several example sentences. Encourage the students to repeat the sentences and to act them out when appropriate.

Teacher Note

Add the word card for *from* to the high-frequency word card review deck.

Monitor the students as they read, and support any student who struggles. When all the students have finished reading, ask and briefly discuss:

Q *What happens in this story?*

Q *Why does Stan get stuck?*

Have the students put their books in their toolboxes. Remind the students that when they go to independent reading, they will read today's book before reading the other books in their toolboxes.

GUIDED SPELLING

fast	"A cheetah runs very fast."
stuck	"My shoe got stuck in the mud."
good	"I hope there is something good for lunch today."

Guide the students through spelling each of the decodable words, paying particular attention to sounds that can be spelled in more than one way. Then have them write the high-frequency word.

Spelling Support

stuck: Remind the students that the sound /k/ at the end of a word is usually spelled *c-k*. Tell the students that in *stuck* the sound /k/ is spelled *c-k*.

Materials

- Teacher and student copies of *The Jug of Water* from Day 2
- Sound card review deck
- High-frequency word card review deck
- Wipe-off board, dry-erase marker, and tissue or cloth
- Group set of the "Individual Reading Observation" sheet (IR1) from Week 1

In this lesson, the students:

- Blend onsets and rimes
- Review spelling-sounds
- Review high-frequency words
- Read a familiar book

1 Phonological Awareness: Blending Onsets and Rimes

Have the students blend each of the following onsets and rimes after you say the phonemes:

/b/ . . . un	bun
/r/ . . . un	run
/s/ . . . un	sun
/f/ . . . un	fun
/st/ . . . un	stun

2 Review Spelling-Sounds

Use the sound card review deck to have the students say the sound of each spelling.

3 Review High-frequency Words

Review the previously introduced high-frequency words by showing each word in the review deck and having the students read it, spell it, and read it again.

4 Reread *The Jug of Water*

Have the students take *The Jug of Water* from their toolboxes and tell them that they will reread this story today. Read the title aloud with the students. Write the word *more* on your wipe-off board, say the word, and remind the students that they will see this word in today's book. Remind them that they will have to remember the word when they see it, or ask for help. Leave the word on your wipe-off board as a reminder and place the board where everyone can see it.

Remind the students that if they finish reading, they will go back to the first page and read the book again. Have the students read *The Jug of Water* in quiet voices.

> **☑ INDIVIDUAL READING OBSERVATION NOTE**
>
> Listen to a few students as they read, taking notes on the "Individual Reading Observation" sheet (IR1) and offering support as needed; see page 144 of the *Assessment Resource Book*.

5 Check Comprehension and Reflect

When all the students have finished reading, ask and briefly discuss:

Q *How do the illustrations help you understand this story?*

Q *What part of the story do you think is funniest? Why?*

Have the students return their books to their toolboxes. Remind the students that when they go to independent reading, they will read today's book before reading the other books in their toolboxes.

GUIDED SPELLING

Stan had a snack.

Guide the students through the sentence, word by word.

Spelling Support

Stan: Remind the students that *Stan* is a name, and that a name always starts with a capital letter.

snack: Remind the students that the sound /k/ at the end of a word is usually spelled *c-k*. Tell the students that in *snack* the sound /k/ is spelled *c-k*.

Week 4

RESOURCES

New

Where Is Mom?

by Rob Arego,
illustrated by Nancy Meyers

Revisit

The Jug of Water

by Rob Arego,
illustrated by Adam Record

Practice or Reteach

The Skunk

by Kenni Alden,
illustrated by Gail Guth

Reteaching

- "Reteach with *The Skunk*"

Assessment Resource Book

- Week 4 assessments

Sound Cards

- *fl* /fl/
- *fr* /fr/
- *_s* /s/, /z/

High-frequency Word Cards

- *for*
- *again*

Wipe-off Boards

 ## Online Resources

Visit the CCC Learning Hub (ccclearninghub.org) to find your online resources for this week.

Assessment Forms

- "Mastery Test 5" record (MT5)
- "Mastery Test 5 Student Card" (SC5)

Reproducibles

- "Set 3, Week 4 Sort" (BLM4)
- (Optional) "High-frequency Words Review 4" (BLM5)

OVERVIEW

Spelling-Sound Focus	High-frequency Words
- fl /fl/	- for
- fr /fr/	- again
- inflectional ending -s /s/, /z/	

⏱ DO AHEAD

✓ Prior to Day 1, add high-frequency word cards for *for* and *again* to the word wall if they are not already displayed.

✓ Prior to Day 2, visit the CCC Learning Hub (ccclearninghub.org) to access and print "Set 3, Week 4 Sort" (BLM4). Make a copy for each student in the group, plus one. Cut apart the pictures on each sheet (keeping one copy intact) to create a set of sorting pictures for middle sounds /ĭ/ and /ŭ/ for each student in the group. Place each set of pictures in a resealable plastic bag.

✓ Prior to Day 3, add the sound cards for *fl, fr* and _s to the sound card review deck.

✓ Prior to Day 3, make a copy of the "Mastery Test 5" record (MT5) for each student in the group; see page 171 of the *Assessment Resource Book*.

✓ Prior to Day 3, make one copy of the "Mastery Test 5 Student Card" (SC5); see page 172 of the *Assessment Resource Book*.

✓ (Optional) If you plan to integrate the new high-frequency words in the word work area, visit the CCC Learning Hub (ccclearninghub.org) to access and print "High-frequency Words Review 4" (BLM5). See "Independent Work Connections" on page 54.

🌐 ELL SUPPORT

- ## fl, fr

  There are words in Spanish with initial *fl* and *fr*, including the cognates *flor* (FLOHR), "flower," and *frente* (FRAYN-tay), "front." However, the letter *r* stands for a stronger trilled sound than the English /r/. There are no equivalent sounds for /fl/ or /fr/ in Korean, Chinese, Vietnamese, or Hmong. Model producing each sound separately. Then have the students blend the sounds together.

- ## s

  The final consonant sound /z/ does not occur in Spanish, Hmong, Korean, or many Chinese dialects. The students may substitute /s/ for /z/. Teach them how to produce /z/ by placing the tongue behind the teeth, forcing air through, and letting the vocal cords vibrate. Help the students compare the sounds by asking them to cover their ears as they pronounce words with final /s/ and final /z/, such as *Gus, has, is, miss, pass, as*.

- ## -s

  There are no plural forms for nouns in Chinese, Vietnamese, or Hmong. In Korean, plural nouns are used only when referring to people. The students may need additional help understanding and correctly using inflectional ending *-s* to signal plurals.

- ## again

  Many English Language Learners have difficulty learning how to stress the appropriate syllable in English words. When you introduce the word *again*, clap the two syllables with the students, marking the syllable division. Repeat the word, stressing the second syllable.

In this lesson, the students:

- Practice oral blending
- Learn the consonant blends *fl* /fl/ and *fr* /fr/
- Read decodable words
- Learn the high-frequency word *for*
- Review high-frequency words
- Read a familiar book

Materials

- Teacher and student copies of *The Jug of Water* from Week 3
- Wipe-off board, dry-erase marker, and tissue or cloth
- High-frequency word card for *for*
- High-frequency word cards review deck

1 Phonological Awareness: Oral Blending

Have the students blend each of the words that follow after you say the phonemes, using continuous blending. Clap softly as you say each sound. Then brush your hands past each other as the students say the word.

/bĕĕsst/	best
/ssnnăăk/	snack
/ffllŏŏp/	flop
/ssnnăăg/	snag
/rrŭŭsst/	rust
/sstŭŭk/	stuck

2 Introduce the Consonant Blends *fl* /fl/ and *fr* /fr/

Explain that today the students will learn two different spellings that they will often see at the beginning of words. Write the spelling *fl* on your wipe-off board. Explain that when the students see the letters *f* and *l* together, they will blend the sounds. Point to the left of *fl* and sweep under the spelling as you say /fl/. Have the students blend the sounds as you sweep under the spelling. Then say each of the words that follow, emphasizing the beginning blend. Have the students repeat each word: *flake, flip, flag.*

Have the students each trace the spelling *fl* on the table in front of them with one finger as they say /fl/.

Repeat the procedure to introduce the consonant blend *fr*, using the words *fresh, from,* and *freeze.*

🌐 ELL Note

Speakers of Spanish and Chinese may have difficulty distinguishing between the blends *fl* and *fr*. Provide the students with practice saying additional *fl* words and *fr* words, such as **fr**og, **fr**uit, **fr**iend, **fl**oat, **fl**ower, and **fl**ag.

Decoding Support

If necessary, support struggling students by covering the ending (including any doubled consonant) and having the students read the base word alone. Then uncover the ending and have them read the entire word. Another option is to write just the base word, have the students read that, double the final consonant if needed, add the ending, and have the students read the inflected word.

🌐 **ELL Note**

English Language Learners may benefit from hearing several example sentences. Encourage the students to repeat the sentences and to act them out when appropriate.

Teacher Note

Add the word card for *for* to the high-frequency word card review deck.

3 Read Decodable Words

Write the following words on your wipe-off board:

Fran	flap
patted	flopping
frog	flat

Point to each word and sweep under it as the students read it.

4 Introduce the High-frequency Word *for*

for   "I picked a flower for you."

Introduce *for* by saying the word as you show the word card to the students. Use the word in a sentence. Have the students read it and spell it twice, and then read it a third time.

5 Review High-frequency Words

Review the previously introduced high-frequency words by showing each word in the review deck and having the students read it, spell it, and read it again.

6 Reread *The Jug of Water*

Have the students take the book *The Jug of Water* from their toolboxes. Tell the students that they will reread this book today. Read the title with the students and ask:

Q *What is funny in this story?*

Have a few volunteers share their thinking with the group. Then have the students read the book in quiet voices.

Monitor the students as they read, and support any student who struggles. When all the students have finished reading, collect the books or have the students return their books to their toolboxes.

GUIDED SPELLING

list   "I always make a grocery list before I go shopping."

flock   "I saw a flock of geese."

water   "Water is good to drink."

Guide the students through spelling each of the decodable words, paying particular attention to sounds that can be spelled in more than one way. Then have them write the high-frequency word.

ELL Note
If necessary, explain that a *flock* is a group of birds or animals, like sheep.

Spelling Support

flock: Remind the students that the sound /k/ at the end of a word is usually spelled *c-k*. Tell the students that in *flock* the sound /k/ is spelled *c-k*.

Where Is Mom?
Oral Segmenting; Inflectional Ending -s and *again*

Day 2

In this lesson, the students:

- Practice oral segmenting
- Learn the spelling-sound of the inflectional ending *-s* /s/, /z/
- Read decodable words
- Learn the high-frequency word *again*
- Review high-frequency words
- Read a new book

1 Phonological Awareness: Oral Segmenting

Have the students segment the phonemes after you say each of the words that follow. Have them clap softly as they say each sound. Then for each word, ask:

Q *How many sounds are in the word* [sniff]?

sniff	/s/ /n/ /ĭ/ /f/
test	/t/ /ĕ/ /s/ /t/
tack	/t/ /ă/ /k/
must	/m/ /ŭ/ /s/ /t/
step	/s/ /t/ /ĕ/ /p/
snip	/s/ /n/ /ĭ/ /p/

Materials

- Teacher and student copies of *Where Is Mom?*
- Wipe-off board, dry-erase marker, and tissue or cloth
- Student bags of sorting pictures, prepared ahead from "Set 3, Week 4 Sort" (BLM4)
- Intact copy of "Set 3, Week 4 Sort" (BLM4), prepared ahead
- High-frequency word card for *again*
- High-frequency word card review deck

2 Introduce the Inflectional Ending -s /s/, /z/

Tell the students that today they will learn about two sounds that the letter *s* stands for at the end of words.

Write the word *cat* on your wipe-off board. Have the students read the word. Then add the letter *s* to the end of the word to make the word *cats*. Point to the word and say *cats*. Tell the students that *cats* means "more than one cat." Point out that the letter *s* in *cats* stands for the sound /s/. Have the students repeat the word as you point to it.

Tell the students that the letter *s* sometimes stands for a different sound at the end of a word. Write *bug* on your wipe-off board. Have the students read the word. Then add the letter *s* to the end of the word to make the word *bugs*. Point to the word and say *bugs*, emphasizing the ending sound /z/. Tell the students that *bugs* means "more than one bug." Have the students repeat the word as you point to it.

Teacher Note

To provide more support, use the same procedure to have the students read more words that end in *s*, such as *nuts*, *mats*, *runs*, *socks*, and *fans*. Have the students name the sound they hear at the end of each word: /s/ or /z/.

3 Read Decodable Words

Write the following words on your wipe-off board:

flops	sniff
ducks	rocks
stems	ruff

Point to each word and sweep under it as the students read it.

4 Introduce the Sound Sort

Display the intact "Set 3, Week 4 Sort" sheet (BLM4) and explain that these are the pictures the students will sort this week. Point to each picture, and say its name. Then have the students say the names as you point to the pictures.

Distribute one bag of sorting pictures to each student. Remind the students that they will sort these pictures into two groups during independent word work. Tell them that one group will have pictures whose names have the middle sound /ĭ/, and the other group will have pictures whose names have the middle sound /ŭ/. Remind them that after they have sorted, they will check their sorts by saying the name of each picture to make sure it is in the right group.

Have the students put their bags in their toolboxes.

Teacher Note

Refer to the picture key for this week's sort. See Appendix B, "Sound Sort Picture Key."

5 Introduce the High-frequency Word *Again*

again   "Please come visit me again."

Introduce *again* by saying the word as you show the word card to the students. Use the word in a sentence. Have the students read it and spell it twice, and then read it a third time.

Teacher Note

Add the word card for *again* to the high-frequency word card review deck.

6 Review High-frequency Words

Review the previously introduced high-frequency words by showing each word in the review deck and having the students read it, spell it, and read it again.

7 Read *Where Is Mom?*

Distribute a copy of *Where Is Mom?* to each student. Tell the students that they will read this book today. Read the title with the students and identify the names of the author and illustrator. Tell the students that this story is about a puppy who is looking for her mother. Open to page 1, and ask the students to find today's new word, *again*. Then turn to page 2, and ask the students to find the new word *for*.

Write the words *bird* and *hears* on your wipe-off board. Read each word as you point to it and have the students say it after you. Tell the students that they will see these words in today's story. Explain that they will have to remember these words when they see them or ask you for help. Leave the words on the wipe-off board as a reminder and place the board where everyone can see them. Have the students turn to page 1 in their books and read the story in quiet voices.

Monitor the students as they read, and support any student who struggles. When all the students have finished reading, ask and briefly discuss:

Q *What happens in this story?*

Q *Where does Fran look for Mom? What does she find?*

Have the students put their books in their toolboxes. Remind the students that when they go to independent reading, they will read today's book before reading the other books in their toolboxes.

GUIDED SPELLING

flap	"A bird can flap its wings."
frog	"A frog can jump very far."
want	"Do you want a snack?"

Guide the students through spelling each of the decodable words, paying particular attention to sounds that can be spelled in more than one way. Then have them write the high-frequency word.

Materials

- Teacher and student copies of *Where Is Mom?* from Day 2
- Sound card review deck
- High-frequency word card review deck
- Wipe-off board, dry-erase marker, and tissue or cloth
- "Mastery Test 5" record (MT5) for each student
- One copy of "Mastery Test 5 Student Card" (SC5)

In this lesson, the students:

- Blend onsets and rimes
- Review spelling-sounds
- Review high-frequency words
- Read a familiar book

1 Phonological Awareness: Blending Onsets and Rimes

Have the students blend each of the following onsets and rimes after you say the phonemes:

/t/ . . . **uck**	tuck
/d/ . . . **uck**	duck
/p/ . . . **uck**	puck
/l/ . . . **uck**	luck
/b/ . . . **uck**	buck
/st/ . . . **uck**	stuck

2 Review Spelling-Sounds

Use the sound card review deck to have the students say the sound of each spelling.

3 Review High-frequency Words

Review the previously introduced high-frequency words by showing each word in the review deck and having the students read it, spell it, and read it again.

4 Reread *Where Is Mom?*

Have the students take *Where Is Mom?* from their toolboxes and tell them that they will reread this story today. Read the title aloud with the students. Write the words *bird* and *hears* on your wipe-off board, say the words, and remind the students that they will see these words in today's book. Remind them that they will have to remember these words when they see them, or ask for help. Leave the word on your wipe-off board as a reminder and place the board where everyone can see it.

Remind the students that if they finish reading, they will go back to the first page and read the book again. Have the students read *Where Is Mom?* in quiet voices.

5 Check Comprehension and Reflect

When all the students have finished reading, ask and briefly discuss:

Q *How does Fran feel at the beginning of the story? How do you know?*

Q *How does Fran feel at the end of the story? How do you know?*

Have the students return their books to their toolboxes. Remind the students that when they go to independent reading, they will read today's book before reading the other books in their tool boxes.

 MASTERY TEST ASSESSMENT NOTE

Administer Mastery Test 5 after this lesson, using "Mastery Test 5" (MT5) and "Mastery Test Student Card" (SC5); see pages 171–172 of the *Assessment Resource Book*.

If you identify students who need to repeat instruction, first determine which sounds and high-frequency words the student missed. Then use "Reteach with *The Good Little Ducks, Part 2*" on page 33 and "Reteach with *The Skunk*" on the next page to reteach needed content. Administer Mastery Test 5 again after reteaching.

GUIDED SPELLING

Did the frog flip?

Guide the students through the sentence, word by word.

Spelling Support

?: Remind the students that a question always ends with a question mark instead of a period.

Teacher Note

You may wish to support your students by showing the illustrations on pages 10 and 14 when you ask these questions.

Teacher Note

You may wish to have students who do not require reteaching put *The Skunk* in their toolboxes for independent reading. If so, introduce the words *bobcat, tail, feet,* and *spring* by writing them on your wipe-off board, saying the words, and explaining that the students will see these words in the book.

Teacher Note

Mastery Test 5 follows this lesson. You may wish to omit Guided Spelling today and use the time to administer mastery tests. Have the students read books from previous weeks during this time.

Teacher Note

If you have students who are struggling to learn the sounds and words you have taught in the previous two weeks, you might provide an additional week of instruction before introducing new sounds and words. For more information, see "Reteaching" in the Introduction.

Teacher Note

Administer Mastery Test 5 again after reteaching. See "Mastery Test Assessment Note" on the previous page.

RETEACHING

Reteach with *The Skunk*

Review the spelling-sounds *sn* /sn/, *st* /st/, *fl* /fl/, *fr* /fr/, the inflectional ending -*s* /s/, /z/, and the high-frequency words *want*, *water*, *from*, *for*, and *again*. Use the book *The Skunk* for reading practice.

Read the title aloud with the students and say that this is a book about a skunk. Write the word *bobcat* on your wipe-off board. Cover *cat* and have the students read *bob*. Then cover *bob* and have the students read *cat*. Then have the students read the whole word. Explain that a bobcat is a wild cat that is bigger than a pet cat but smaller than a lion and that the students will see this word in their book. Show the picture of the bobcat on page 10. Write the words *tail*, *feet*, and *spring* on your wipe-off board, say the words, and have the students say them. Explain that the students will see these words in today's book. Tell the students that they will have to remember these words when they see them, or ask you for help. Leave the words on your wipe-off board as a reminder and place the board where everyone can see it.

Explain that the students will read the book in quiet voices. Review that students who finish reading early will go back to the first page and read the book again. Have the students read *The Skunk*.

When all the students have finished reading, ask and briefly discuss:

Q *What did you find out about skunks from this book?*

Collect the books or have the students put their books in their toolboxes.

Independent Work Connections

▪ You may wish to use "High-frequency Words Review 4" (BLM5) to have the students practice high-frequency words using any activities you have introduced. If you decide to add these words, we recommend printing them on colored paper or identifying them by color in another way (for example, by using colored dots or colored baskets). Show these to the students and tell them which color set of words to use during independent word work.

RESOURCES

New

Drip Drop

by Erica J. Green,
illustrated by Jess Golden

Revisit

Where Is Mom?

by Rob Arego,
illustrated by Nancy Meyers

Assessment Resource Book
- Week 5 assessment

Sound Cards
- *gr* /gr/
- *dr* /dr/

High-frequency Word Cards
- *many*
- *people*

Wipe-off Boards

 ## Online Resources

Visit the CCC Learning Hub (ccclearninghub.org) to find your online resources for this week.

Assessment Form
- "Individual Reading Observation" sheet (IR1)

Reproducible
- "Set 3, Week 5 Sort" (BLM6)

OVERVIEW

Spelling-Sound Focus	High-frequency Words
• gr /gr/	• *many*
• dr /dr/	• *people*

⏱ DO AHEAD

✓ Prior to Day 1, add high-frequency word cards for *many* and *people* to the word wall if they are not already displayed.

✓ Prior to Day 2, visit the CCC Learning Hub (ccclearninghub.org) to access and print "Set 3, Week 5 Sort" (BLM6). Make a copy for each student in the group, plus two. Cut apart the pictures on each sheet (keeping one copy intact) to create a set of sorting pictures for rimes *an* and *at* for each student in the group and one for yourself. Place each set of pictures in a resealable plastic bag.

✓ Prior to Day 3, add the sound cards for *gr* and *dr* to the sound card review deck.

🌐 ELL SUPPORT

• **gr, dr**

There are words in Spanish with initial *gr* and *dr*, including the cognates *grupo* (GROO-poh), "group," and *dragón* (dra-GOHN), "dragon." However, the letter *r* stands for a stronger trilled sound than the English /r/.

• **gr, dr**

There are no initial consonant blends in Chinese. The students may insert a slight vowel sound between the consonants.

• **gr, dr**

There are no equivalents for the combined sounds /gr/ or /dr/ in Korean, Chinese, Vietnamese, or Hmong. Model producing each sound separately. Then have the students blend the sounds together.

(continues)

🌐 ELL SUPPORT   *(continued)*

▪ **people**

Many English Language Learners have difficulty pronouncing words that end with consonant-*l-e*. Write the word *people* where the students can see it and mark the syllable juncture between the two syllables: *peo-ple*. Say one syllable at a time and have the students repeat it. Then model saying the entire word. If necessary, have the students repeat the consonant-*l-e* syllable several times.

In this lesson, the students:

- Practice oral blending
- Learn the consonant blend *gr* /gr/
- Read decodable words
- Learn the high-frequency word *many*
- Review high-frequency words
- Read a familiar book

Materials

- Teacher and student copies of *Where Is Mom?* from Week 4
- Wipe-off board, dry-erase marker, and tissue or cloth
- High-frequency word card for *many*
- High-frequency word card review deck

1 Phonological Awareness: Oral Blending

Have the students blend each of the words that follow after you say the phonemes, using continuous blending. Clap softly as you say each sound. Then brush your hands past each other as the students say the word.

/ffrrĕĕsh/	fresh
/ffllăăt/	flat
/ffrrŏŏg/	frog
/ffllăăg/	flag
/mmŏŏpss/	mops
/ffllăăsh/	flash
/pĕĕtss/	pets

2 Introduce the Consonant Blend *gr* /gr/

Explain that today the students will learn a pair of letters that they will often see at the beginning of words. Write the spelling *gr* on your wipe-off board. Explain that when the students see the letters *g* and *r* together, they will blend the sounds. Point to the left of *gr* and sweep under the spelling as you say /gr/. Have the students blend the sounds as you sweep under the spelling. Then say the words that follow, emphasizing the beginning blend. Have the students repeat each word: *grape, grin, grab*.

Have the students each trace the spelling *gr* on the table in front of them with one finger as they say /gr/.

3 ## Read Decodable Words

Write the following words on your wipe-off board:

Gran	grip
gripping	flip
grass	flat

Point to each word and sweep under it as the students read it.

4 ## Introduce the High-frequency Word *Many*

many   "There are many kinds of fruit."

Introduce *many* by saying the word as you show the word card to the students. Use the word in a sentence. Have the students read it and spell it twice, and then read it a third time.

5 ## Review High-frequency Words

Review the previously introduced high-frequency words by showing each word in the review deck and having the students read it, spell it, and read it again.

6 ## Reread *Where Is Mom?*

Have the students take the book *Where Is Mom?* from their toolboxes. Tell the students that they will reread this book today. Read the title with the students and ask:

Q *What do you remember about this story?*

Have a few volunteers share their thinking with the group. Then have the students read the book in quiet voices.

Monitor the students as they read, and support any student who struggles. When all the students have finished reading, collect the books or have the students return their books to their toolboxes.

GUIDED SPELLING

grip	"Grip the bat tightly when you hit the ball."
flap	"The duck will flap its wings to take off from the pond."
for	"I brought a sandwich to eat for lunch."

Guide the students through spelling each of the decodable words, paying particular attention to sounds that can be spelled in more than one way. Then have them write the high-frequency word.

In this lesson, the students:

- Practice oral segmenting

- Learn the consonant blend *dr* /dr/

- Read decodable words

- Identify rhyming sounds for the sound sort

- Learn the high-frequency word *people*

- Review high-frequency words

- Read a new book

Materials

- Teacher and student copies of *Drip Drop*

- Wipe-off board, dry-erase marker, and tissue or cloth

- Teacher and student bags of sorting pictures, prepared ahead from "Set 3, Week 5 Sort" (BLM6)

- Intact copy of "Set 3, Week 5 Sort" (BLM6), prepared ahead

- High-frequency word card for *people*

- High-frequency word card review deck

1 Phonological Awareness: Oral Segmenting

Have the students segment the phonemes after you say each of the words that follow. Have them clap softly as they say each sound. Then for each word, ask:

Q *How many sounds are in the word [flag]?*

flag	/f/ /l/ /ă/ /g/
Fran	/f/ /r /ă/ /n/
casts	/k/ /ă/ /s/ /t/ /s/
flop	/f/ /l/ /ŏ/ /p/
bud	/b/ /ŭ/ /d/
frill	/f/ /r/ /ĭ/ /l/

2 Introduce the Consonant Blend *dr* /dr/

Explain that today the students will learn a pair of letters that they will often see together at the beginning of words. Write the spelling *dr* on your wipe-off board. Explain that when the students see the letters *d* and *r* together, they will blend the sounds. Point to the left of *dr* and sweep under the spelling as you say /dr/. Have the students blend the sounds as you sweep under the spelling. Then say each of the words that follow, emphasizing the beginning blend. Have the students repeat each word: *drip, drop, drink*.

Have the students each trace the spelling *dr* on the table in front of them with one finger as they say /dr/.

3 Read Decodable Words

Write the following words on your wipe-off board:

drip	drag
drops	buds
flapped	frog

Point to each word and sweep under it as the students read it.

4 Introduce the Sound Sort

Remind the students that they have been sorting pictures by the first sounds, last sounds, and middle sounds in their names. Explain that this week they will sort pictures with names that rhyme. Display the intact "Set 3, Week 5 Sort" sheet (BLM6) and explain that these are the pictures the students will sort this week. Point to each picture and say its name. Then have the students say the names as you point to the pictures.

Teacher Note

Refer to the picture key for this week's sort. See Appendix B, "Sound Sort Picture Key."

Take the sorting guide from your own bag of pictures and hold it up. Point out the arrow on the sorting guide (the first square on BLM6). Explain that the arrow pointing to the box on the sorting guide means that the students will sort by rhyming sounds. Then point to the pictures of the fan and the cat on the sorting guide and explain that these pictures show the rhyming sounds the students will match (in this case, *an* and *at*).

Place your sorting guide on the table in front of you. Point to the picture of the fan and say: *fan, an.* Then point to the picture of the cat and say: *cat, at.* Hold up the *hat* picture from your bag. Ask:

Q *What sounds do you hear at the end of* hat? *Does* hat *rhyme with* cat *or with* fan?

Teacher Note

If necessary, support the students in identifying rhymes by repeating the question for other pictures on the sheet of sorting pictures.

Confirm that *hat* rhymes with *cat* and model placing the picture below the *cat* picture. Practice the procedure again, using the *man* picture.

Distribute one bag of sorting pictures to each student. Have the students first find the sorting guide and place it on the table. Remind them that the arrow pointing to the box will remind them to sort by rhyming sounds. Review that the pictures of the fan and the cat show that they will sort by the rhyming sounds *an* and *at*.

Ask each student to choose one picture from his bag, say the name of the picture quietly to himself, and decide whether the word rhymes with *at* or *an*. Review that if the word rhymes with *an*, he will put the picture below the *fan* picture; if it rhymes with *at*, he will put it below the *cat* picture. Support the students as necessary.

When all the students have placed at least one picture, tell them that they will now check their work. Explain that they will say the name of the picture to themselves and listen carefully to what they say. If they have put a picture in the wrong place, they can move it. Model by checking the *man* picture. Point to the *man* picture and say: *man.* Ask:

Q *Does* man *rhyme with* an? *Is the* man *picture in the right place?*

Have each student check his picture and move it if necessary. Then have the students check any additional pictures they sorted.

Tell the students that if they need help remembering how to sort their pictures during independent word work, they may quietly ask another student in their reading group to remind them. Have them put their sorting pictures in their bags and put the bags in their toolboxes.

5 Introduce the High-frequency Word *People*

people   "There were many people on the bus this morning."

Introduce *people* by saying the word as you show the word card to the students. Use the word in a sentence. Have the students read it and spell it twice, and then read it a third time.

6 Review High-frequency Words

Review the previously introduced high-frequency words by showing each word in the review deck and having the students read it, spell it, and read it again.

7 Read *Drip Drop*

Distribute a copy of *Drip Drop* to each student. Tell the students that they will read this book today. Read the title with the students and identify the names of the author and illustrator. Tell the students that this story is about a problem and how the problem is fixed. Open to page 1, and ask the students to find the new word *many.* Then to page 2, and ask the students to find today's new word, *people.*

Write the word *bud* on your wipe-off board and have the students read the word. Point to the buds in the illustration on page 1, and explain that a *bud* is a flower that hasn't opened yet. Write the words *new* and *hose* on your wipe-off board. Read each word as you point to it and have the students say it after you. Tell the students that they will see these words in today's story. Explain that they will have to remember these words when they see them, or ask you for help. Leave the words on the wipe-off board as a reminder and place the board where everyone can see it. Have the students turn to page 1 in their books and read the story in quiet voices.

Teacher Note

Add the word card for *people* to the high-frequency word card review deck.

Teacher Note

You may wish to draw a hose and a bud next to the words.

Monitor the students as they read, and support any student who struggles. When all the students have finished reading, ask and briefly discuss:

Q *Why does Gran need the hose?*

Q *What happens in the story?*

Have the students put their books in their toolboxes. Remind the students that when they go to independent reading, they will read today's book before reading the other books in their toolboxes.

GUIDED SPELLING

drip	"Rain will drip from the sky."
buds	"The flower buds will open soon."
again	"We will read again tomorrow."

Guide the students through spelling each of the decodable words, paying particular attention to sounds that can be spelled in more than one way. Then have them write the high-frequency word.

Spelling Support

buds: Support the students in writing the base word, *bud*, before adding the inflectional ending to write *buds*.

In this lesson, the students:

- Blend onsets and rimes
- Review spelling-sounds
- Review high-frequency words
- Read a familiar book

1 Phonological Awareness: Blending Onsets and Rimes

Have the students blend each of the following onsets and rimes after you say the phonemes:

/b/ . . . **all**	ball
/f/ . . . **all**	fall
/w/ . . . **all**	wall
/t/ . . . **all**	tall
/h/ . . . **all**	hall
/k/ . . . **all**	call

2 Review Spelling-Sounds

Use the sound card review deck to have the students say the sound of each spelling.

3 Review High-frequency Words

Review the previously introduced high-frequency words by showing each word in the review deck and having the students read it, spell it, and read it again.

4 Reread *Drip Drop*

Have the students take *Drip Drop* from their toolboxes and tell them that they will reread this story today. Read the title aloud with the students. Write the words *new* and *hose* on your wipe-off board, say the words, have the students say them, and remind the students that they will see these words in today's book. Remind them that they will have to remember these words when they see them, or ask for help. Leave the words on the wipe-off board and place the board where everyone can see it.

Materials

- Teacher and student copies of *Drip Drop* from Day 2
- Sound card review deck
- High-frequency word card review deck
- Wipe-off board, dry-erase marker, and tissue or cloth
- Group set of the "Individual Reading Observation" sheet (IR1) from Week 3

Teacher Note

Build the review deck by adding the sound cards for the sounds you introduce to the group. After you have accumulated about 20 cards, begin removing cards for spelling-sounds the students know well.

Remind the students that if they finish reading, they will go back to the first page and read the book again. Have the students read *Drip Drop* in quiet voices.

INDIVIDUAL READING OBSERVATION NOTE

Listen to a few students as they read, taking notes on the "Individual Reading Observation" sheet (IR1) and offering support as needed; see page 144 of the *Assessment Resource Book*.

5 Check Comprehension and Reflect

When all the students have finished reading, ask and briefly discuss:

Q *When have you needed help doing something? Who helped you?*

Have the students return their books to their toolboxes. Remind the students that when they go to independent reading, they will read today's book before reading the other books in their toolboxes.

GUIDED SPELLING

Water can drip.

Guide the students through the sentence, word by word.

RESOURCES

New

Revisit

Practice or Reteach

Make Plum Jam

by Erica J. Green,
illustrated by
Marjorie Leggitt

Drip Drop

by Erica J. Green,
illustrated by Jess Golden

The Band

by Elizabeth Johnson,
illustrated by Jess Golden

Reteaching
- "Reteach with *The Band*"

Assessment Resource Book
- Week 6 assessment

Sound Cards
- *pl* /pl/
- *sm* /sm/

High-frequency Word Cards
- *your*
- *very*

Wipe-off Boards

 ## Online Resources

Visit the CCC Learning Hub (ccclearninghub.org) to find your online resources for this week.

Assessment Form
- "Group Progress Assessment" sheet (GA2)

Reproducible
- "Set 3, Week 6 Sort" (BLM7)

OVERVIEW

Spelling-Sound Focus
- *pl* /pl/
- *sm* /sm/

High-frequency Words
- *your*
- *very*

⏱ DO AHEAD

✓ Prior to Day 1, add high-frequency word cards for *your* and *very* to the word wall if they are not already displayed.

✓ Prior to Day 2, visit the CCC Learning Hub (ccclearninghub.org) to access and print "Set 3, Week 6 Sort" (BLM7). Make a copy for each student in the group, plus one. Cut apart the pictures on each sheet (keeping one copy intact) to create a set of sorting pictures for the rimes *in* and *ing* for each student in the group. Place each set of pictures in a resealable plastic bag.

✓ Prior to Day 3, add the sound cards for *pl* and *sm* to the sound card review deck.

✓ Prior to Day 3, make a copy of the "Group Progress Assessment" sheet (GA2); see page 169 of the *Assessment Resource Book*.

🌐 ELL SUPPORT

- **pl**

  There are words in Spanish with initial *pl*, including the cognates *plan* (PLAN), "plan," and *planta* (PLAN-tah), "plant."

- **sm**

  There are no initial or final *s* blends in Spanish. The spelling *sm* only occurs in separate syllables, such as in *esmeralda* (ehs-mair-AHL-dah), "emerald." The students may add a vowel sound before the initial consonant in words that begin with *sm*.

(continues)

🌐 ELL SUPPORT *(continued)*

- **pl, sm**

  There are no equivalents for the combined sounds /pl/ or /sm/ in Korean, Chinese, Vietnamese, or Hmong. Model producing each sound separately. Then have the students blend the sounds together.

In this lesson, the students:

- Practice oral blending
- Learn the consonant blend *pl* /pl/
- Read decodable words
- Learn the high-frequency word *your*
- Review high-frequency words
- Read a familiar book

Materials

- Teacher and student copies of *Drip Drop* from Week 5
- Wipe-off board, dry-erase marker, and tissue or cloth
- High-frequency word card for *your*
- High-frequency word cards review deck

1 Phonological Awareness: Oral Blending

Have the students blend each of the words that follow after you say the phonemes, using continuous blending. Clap softly as you say each sound. Then brush your hands past each other as the students say the word.

/pllăănn/	plan
/pllŏŏp/	plop
/ffĭĭtss/	fits
/pllŭŭmm/	plum
/pllŭŭk/	pluck
/llăăpss/	laps

2 Introduce the Consonant Blend *pl* /pl/

Explain that today the students will learn a pair of letters that they will often see together at the beginning of words. Write the spelling *pl* on your wipe-off board. Explain that when the students see the letters *p* and *l* together, they will blend the sounds. Point to the left of *pl* and sweep under the spelling as you say /pl/. Have the students blend the sounds as you sweep under the spelling. Then say each of the words that follow, emphasizing the beginning blend. Have the students repeat each word: *please, plate, plug.*

Have the students each trace the spelling *pl* on the table in front of them with one finger as they say /pl/.

3 Read Decodable Words

Write the following words on your wipe-off board:

plums	plan
mixed	plop
drum	flag

Point to each word and sweep under it as the students read it.

4 Introduce the High-frequency Word *Your*

your   "What is your name?"

Introduce *your* by saying the word as you show the word card to the students. Use the word in a sentence. Have the students read it and spell it twice, and then read it a third time.

Teacher Note

Add the word card for *your* to the high-frequency word card review deck.

5 Review High-frequency Words

Review the previously introduced high-frequency words by showing each word in the review deck and having the students read it, spell it, and read it again.

6 Reread *Drip Drop*

Have the students take the book *Drip Drop* from their toolboxes. Tell the students that they will reread this book today. Read the title with the students and ask:

Q *What is funny about this story?*

Have a few volunteers share their thinking with the group. Then have the students read the book in quiet voices.

Monitor the students as they read, and support any student who struggles. When all the students have finished reading, collect the books or have the students return their books to their toolboxes.

GUIDED SPELLING

plum	"A plum is a fruit."
plan	"We made a plan to go to the library on Saturday."
many	"I like many kinds of fruit."

Guide the students through spelling each of the decodable words, paying particular attention to sounds that can be spelled in more than one way. Then have them write the high-frequency word.

In this lesson, the students:

- Practice oral segmenting
- Learn the consonant blend *sm* /sm/
- Read decodable words
- Learn the high-frequency word *very*
- Review high-frequency words
- Read a new book

1 Phonological Awareness: Oral Segmenting

Have the students segment the phonemes after you say each of the following words:

stack	/s/ /t/ /ă/ /k/
smell	/s/ /m/ /ĕ/ /l/
pots	/p/ /ŏ/ /t/ /s/
smash	/s/ /m/ /ă/ /sh/
naps	/n/ /ă/ /p/ /s/
smock	/s/ /m/ /ŏ/ /k/

2 Introduce the Consonant Blend *sm* /sm/

Explain that today the students will learn a pair of letters that they will often see together at the beginning of words. Write the spelling *sm* on your wipe-off board. Explain that when the students see the letters *s* and *m* together, they will blend the sounds. Point to the left of *sm* and sweep under the spelling as you say /sm/. Have the students blend the sounds as you sweep under the spelling. Then say each of the words that follow, emphasizing the beginning blend. Have the students repeat each word: *smile*, *smudge*, *small*.

Have the students each trace the spelling *sm* on the table in front of them with one finger as they say /sm/.

Materials

- Teacher and students copies of *Make Plum Jam*
- Wipe-off board, dry-erase marker, and tissue or cloth
- Student bags of sorting pictures, prepared ahead from "Set 3, Week 6 Sort" (BLM7)
- Intact copy of "Set 3, Week 6 Sort" (BLM7), prepared ahead
- High-frequency word card for *very*
- High-frequency word card review deck

Teacher Note

You may wish to explain that a *smock* is a kind of jacket or coat that is worn to protect clothing from paint or other messy things.

ELL Note

You may wish to have the students practice saying additional words beginning with *sm*, such as **sm**ell, **sm**art, **sm**oke.

3 Read Decodable Words

Write the following words on your wipe-off board:

smack	smash
back	smudge
drilled	flapping

Point to each word and sweep under it as the students read it.

4 Introduce the Sound Sort

Display the intact "Set 3, Week 6 Sort" sheet (BLM7), and explain that these are the pictures the students will sort this week. Point to each picture and say its name. Then have the students say the names as you point to the pictures.

Distribute one bag of sorting pictures to each student. Remind the students that they will sort these pictures into two groups during independent word work. Tell them that one group will have pictures whose names rhyme with *ring*, and the other group will have pictures whose names rhyme with *pin*. Remind them that after they have sorted, they will check their sorts by saying the name of each picture to make sure it is in the right group.

Have the students put their bags in their toolboxes.

5 Introduce the High-frequency Word *Very*

very   "It is very warm today."

Introduce *very* by saying the word as you show the word card to the students. Use the word in a sentence. Have the students read it and spell it twice, and then read it a third time.

6 Review High-frequency Words

Review the previously introduced high-frequency words by showing each word in the review deck and having the students read it, spell it, and read it again.

7 Read *Make Plum Jam*

Distribute a copy of *Make Plum Jam* to each student. Tell the students that they will read this book today. Read the title with the students and identify the names of the author and illustrator. Ask:

Q *What do you think this book is about?*

Have a few volunteers share their thinking with the group.

Open to page 1, and ask the students to find today's new word, *very*. Then turn to page 2, and ask the students to find the new word *your*.

Write the word *plot* on your wipe-off board and read the word with the students. Explain that a *plot* is a small piece of land that is used as a garden. Write the words *smidge* and *smudge* on your wipe-off board and blend and read them with the students. Explain that a *smidge* of something is a little bit of it. Then explain that when you *smudge* something, you make it dirty. Write the word *make* on your wipe-off board and have the students read the word. Write *take* immediately below *make* and tell the students that this word rhymes with the word *make*, which they know, but it begins with the sound /t/. Have the students say *take*. Explain that they will see this word in the book today, and they will have to notice that it rhymes with *make* when they come to it.

Then write the words *sugar*, *stir*, and *adult* on your wipe-off board and read them for the students. Have the students say the words. Tell the students that they will see these words in today's book. Explain that they will have to remember these words when they see them, or ask you for help. Leave the words on the wipe-off board as a reminder and place the board where everyone can see it. Then have the students turn to page 1 in their books and read the story in quiet voices.

Monitor the students as they read, and support any student who struggles. When all the students have finished reading, ask and briefly discuss:

Q *What did you find out about making jam?*

Have the students put their books in their toolboxes. Remind them that when they go to independent reading, they will read today's book before reading the other books in their toolboxes.

GUIDED SPELLING

smell	"I like the way roses smell."
stop	"We will stop class to eat lunch at 11:45."
people	"People need food and water to live."

Guide the students through spelling each of the decodable words, paying particular attention to sounds that can be spelled in more than one way. Then have them write the high-frequency word.

Spelling Support

smell: Tell the students that the sound /l/ at the end of a word is usually spelled *l-l*. Tell the students that in *smell* the sound /l/ is spelled *l-l*.

Materials

- Teacher and student copies of *Make Plum Jam* from Day 2
- Sound card review deck
- High-frequency word card review deck
- Wipe-off board, dry-erase marker, and tissue or cloth
- "Group Progress Assessment" sheet (GA2)

In this lesson, the students:

- Produce rhymes
- Review spelling-sounds
- Review high-frequency words
- Read a familiar book

1 Phonological Awareness: Producing Rhymes

Tell the students that today they will make words that rhyme. Ask:

Q *What do you know about rhymes?*

Q *What are some words that rhyme?*

Have a few volunteers share their thinking with the group.

Explain that the students will say words that rhyme with *at*. You will say the first sound and the students will make a word that begins with that sound and rhymes with *at*. Model, using the sound /s/. Say *at*. Then say /s/. Blend the sounds to say the word, /s/ . . . /at/, *sat*. Say the two rhyming words (*at*, *sat*) and have the students repeat the words. Ask:

Q *Does* sat *rhyme with* at?

Confirm that *sat* rhymes with *at*. Have the students add each of the following first sounds to *at* to make rhyming words:

/b/	(bat)
/f/	(fat)
/h/	(hat)
/m/	(mat)
/r/	(rat)
/p/	(pat)

> **You might say:**
>
> "Rhyme these sounds with *at*: /b/ (*bat*), /f/ (*fat*)."

2 Review Spelling-Sounds

Use the sound card review deck to have the students say the sound of each spelling.

3 Review High-frequency Words

Review the previously introduced high-frequency words by showing each word in the review deck and having the students read it, spell it, and read it again.

4 Reread *Make Plum Jam*

Have the students take *Make Plum Jam* from their toolboxes and tell them that they will reread this book today. Read the title aloud with the students. Write the words *take*, *sugar*, *stir*, and *adult* on your wipe-off board, say the words, and remind the students that they will see these words in today's book. Remind them that they will have to remember these words when they see them, or ask you for help. Leave the words on the wipe-off board as a reminder and place the board where everyone can see it.

Remind the students that if they finish reading, they will go back to the first page and read the book again. Have the students read *Make Plum Jam* in quiet voices.

 GROUP PROGRESS ASSESSMENT NOTE

As you observe the group, ask yourself:

- Can the students produce rhyming words?
- Did the group understand the steps in making jam?

Record your observations on the "Group Progress Assessment" sheet (GA2); see page 169 of the *Assessment Resource Book*. Support struggling students by reteaching previous content; see "Reteach with *The Band*" on the next page. If the students struggle with rhyming, provide additional practice by repeating the phonological awareness activity with another rime (see Day 1, Step 2).

Teacher Note

You may wish to have students who do not require reteaching put *The Band* in their toolboxes for independent reading. If so, introduce the words *play* and *show* by writing them on your wipe-off board, saying the words, and explaining that the students will see these words in the book.

---

5 Check Comprehension and Reflect

When all the students have finished reading, ask and briefly discuss:

Q *What do you do to make jam?*

Q *Do you think it is easy or hard to make plum jam? Why?*

Have the students return their books to their toolboxes. Remind them that when they go to independent reading, they will read today's book before reading the other books in their toolboxes.

GUIDED SPELLING

Are plums good?

Guide the students through the sentence, word by word.

Spelling Support

Support the students in writing the base word, *plum*, before adding the inflectional ending to write *plums*.

?: Remind the students that a question always ends with a question mark instead of a period.

RETEACHING

Reteach with *The Band*

Review the consonant blends *gr* /gr/, *dr* /dr/, *pl* /pl/, and *sm* /sm/, and the high-frequency words *many*, *people*, *your*, and *very*. Use *The Band* for reading practice.

After reading the title aloud with the students, write the words *play* and *show* on your wipe-off board, say the words, and have the students say them. Explain that the students will see these words in today's book. Tell the students that they will have to remember these words when they see them, or ask you for help. Leave the words on the wipe-off board as a reminder and place the board where everyone can see it.

Explain that the students will read the book in quiet voices. Review that students who finish reading early will go back to the first page and read the book again. Have the students read *The Band*.

When all the students have finished reading, ask and briefly discuss:

Q *What happens first in this book? Next? At the end?*

Collect the books or have the students put their books in their toolboxes.

Teacher Note

If you have students who are struggling to learn the sounds and words you have taught in the previous two weeks, you might provide an additional week of instruction before introducing new sounds and words. For more information, see "Reteaching" in the Introduction.

RESOURCES

New

Revisit

The Spelling Test

by Rob Arego,
illustrated by Linda Pierce

Make Plum Jam

by Erica J. Green,
illustrated by
Marjorie Leggitt

Assessment Resource Book

- Week 7 assessment

Sound Cards

- *sp* /sp/
- *cl* /kl/

High-frequency Word Cards

- *could*
- *would*
- *should*
- *were*

Wipe-off Boards

 ## Online Resources

Visit the CCC Learning Hub (ccclearninghub.org) to find your online resources for this week.

Assessment Form

- "Individual Reading Observation" sheet (IR1)

Reproducible

- "Set 3, Week 7 Sort" (BLM8)

OVERVIEW

Spelling-Sound Focus	High-frequency Words
▪ *sp* /sp/	▪ *could*
▪ *cl* /kl/	▪ *would*
	▪ *should*
	▪ *were*

⏱ DO AHEAD

✓ Prior to Day 1, add high-frequency word cards for *could*, *would*, *should*, and *were* to the word wall if they are not already displayed.

✓ Prior to Day 2, visit the CCC Learning Hub (ccclearninghub.org) to access and print "Set 3, Week 7 Sort" (BLM8). Make a copy for each student in the group, plus two. Cut apart the pictures on each sheet (keeping one copy intact) to create a set of sorting pictures with rhyming pairs for each student in the group and one for yourself. Place each set of pictures in a resealable plastic bag.

✓ Prior to Day 3, add the sound cards for *sp* and *cl* to the sound card review deck.

🌐 ELL SUPPORT

▪ cl

There are words in Spanish with initial *cl*, including the cognates *club*, "club" (KLUB), and *clima* (KLEE-mah), "climate."

▪ sp

There are no initial or final *s* blends in Spanish. The spelling *sp* only occurs in separate syllables, such as in *espero* (ehs-PAIR-oh), "I hope." The students may add a vowel sound before the initial consonant in words that begin with *sp* and after the final consonant in words that end with *sp*.

(continues)

🌐 ELL SUPPORT *(continued)*

• could, would, should

Even students with advanced levels of English proficiency have difficulty understanding all the different uses of the modals *could*, *would*, and *should*. Spend some time explaining how the words are used in different contexts. *Could* and *would* tell about things that are possible or likely to happen. *Would* is also used in polite questions. *Should* means that something is necessary or important to do. Have pairs of students work together to use each word in a question-and-answer format.

Make Plum Jam
Oral Blending;
sp; *could*, *would*, and *should*

Day 1

In this lesson, the students:

- Practice oral blending
- Learn the consonant blend *sp* /sp/
- Read decodable words
- Learn the high-frequency words *could*, *would*, and *should*
- Review high-frequency words
- Read a familiar book

1 Phonological Awareness: Oral Blending

Have the students blend each of the following words after you say the phonemes, using continuous blending:

/sspĭĭll/	spill
/pllăănn/	plan
/sspĕĕk/	speck
/pllŭŭk/	pluck
/sspĭĭnn/	spin
/pllŏŏp/	plop

2 Introduce the Consonant Blend *sp* /sp/

Explain that today the students will learn a pair of letters that they will often see together at the beginning of words. Write the spelling *sp* on your wipe-off board. Explain that when the students see the letters *s* and *p* together, they will blend the sounds. Point to the left of *sp* and sweep under the spelling as you say /sp/. Have the students blend the sounds as you sweep under the spelling. Then say each of the words that follow, emphasizing the beginning blend. Have the students repeat each word: ***sp**in*, ***sp**ace*, ***sp**ell*.

Tell the students that they will also see *s* and *p* together at the end of words. Say each of the words that follow, emphasizing the ending blend. Have the students repeat each word: *ga**sp**, li**sp**, wi**sp***.

Have the students each trace the spelling *sp* on the table in front of them with one finger as they say /sp/.

Materials

- Teacher and student copies of *Make Plum Jam* from Week 6
- Wipe-off board, dry-erase marker, and tissue or cloth
- High-frequency word card for *could*
- High-frequency word card for *would*
- High-frequency word card for *should*
- High-frequency word card review deck

 ELL Note

You may wish to have the students practice saying additional words beginning with *sp*, such as ***sp**oon*, ***sp**ot*, and ***sp**eak*.

Decoding Support

If necessary, support struggling students by covering the ending (including any doubled consonant) and having the students read the base word alone. Then uncover the ending and have them read the entire word. Another option is to write just the base word, have the students read that, double the final consonant if needed, add the ending, and have the students read the inflected word.

Teacher Note

Add the word cards for *could*, *would*, and *should* to the high-frequency word card review deck.

3 Read Decodable Words

Write the following words on your wipe-off board:

spell	spelling
flag	spot
slipped	list

Point to each word and sweep under it as the students read it.

4 Introduce the High-frequency Words *Could, Would,* and *Should*

could	"We could fly if we had wings."
would	"I would like to travel some day."
should	"We should eat lots of fruit and vegetables."

Explain that today the students will learn three high-frequency words that rhyme. Introduce *could*, *would*, and *should* by saying each word as you show the word card to the students. Use the word in a sentence. Have the students read it and spell it twice, and then read it a third time. Then write all three words where the students can see them and underline the common letters. Have the students read all three words again.

5 Review High-frequency Words

Review the previously introduced high-frequency words by showing each word in the review deck and having the students read it, spell it, and read it again.

6 Reread *Make Plum Jam*

Have the students take the book *Make Plum Jam* from their toolboxes. Tell the students that they will reread this book today. Read the title with the students and ask:

Q *What do you remember about making jam?*

Have a few volunteers share their thinking with the group. Then have the students read the story in quiet voices.

Monitor the students as they read, and support any student who struggles. When all the students have finished reading, collect the books or have the students return their books to their toolboxes.

GUIDED SPELLING

plot	"I grow tomatoes in my garden plot."
test	"The doctor gave me an eye test to see whether I needed glasses."
your	"What is your favorite game to play at recess?"

Guide the students through spelling each of the decodable words, paying particular attention to sounds that can be spelled in more than one way. Then have them write the high-frequency word.

The Spelling Test
Oral Segmenting; *cl* and *were*

Day 2

In this lesson, the students:

- Practice oral segmenting
- Learn the consonant blend *cl* /kl/
- Read decodable words
- Identify rhyming words for the sound sort
- Learn the high-frequency word *were*
- Review high-frequency words
- Read a new book

Materials

- Teacher and student copies of *The Spelling Test*
- Wipe-off board, dry-erase marker, and tissue or cloth
- Teacher and student bags of sorting pictures, prepared ahead from "Set 3, Week 7 Sort" (BLM8)
- Intact copy of "Set 3, Week 7 Sort" (BLM8), prepared ahead
- High-frequency word card for *were*
- High-frequency word card review deck

1 Phonological Awareness: Oral Segmenting

Have the students segment the phonemes after you say each of the words that follow. Have them clap softly as they say each sound.

plum	/p/ /l/ /ŭ/ /m/
spun	/s/ /p/ /ŭ/ /n/
plan	/p/ /l/ /ă/ /n/
spot	/s/ /p/ /ŏ/ /t/
pledge	/p/ /l/ /ĕ/ /j/
span	/s/ /p/ /ă/ /n/

2 Introduce the Consonant Blend *cl* /kl/

Explain that today the students will learn a pair of letters that they will often see together at the beginning of words. Write the letters *cl* on your wipe-off board. Explain that when the students see the letters *c* and *l* together, they will blend the sounds. Point to the left of *cl* and sweep under the spelling as you say /kl/. Have the students blend the sounds as you sweep under the spelling. Then say each of the words that follow, emphasizing the beginning blend. Have the students repeat each word: *clock, clean, class*.

Have the students each trace the letters *cl* on the table in front of them with one finger as they say /kl/.

3 Read Decodable Words

Write the following words on your wipe-off board:

class	will
clock	shut
Cliff	them

Point to each word and sweep under it as the students read it.

4 Introduce the Sound Sort

Teacher Note

Point out that *Cliff* is a name. You might also draw a picture of a cliff and explain that *cliff* can also mean a very steep hill.

Remind the students that so far they have been sorting pictures into groups, using a sorting guide. Tell the students that today they will sort pictures into pairs, and they will not use a sorting guide. Explain that they will find pictures with names that rhyme and that they will make rhyming pairs with these pictures.

Display the intact "Set 3, Week 7 Sort" sheet (BLM8) and explain that these are the pictures the students will sort today. Point to each picture and say its name. Then have the students say the names as you point to the pictures.

Teacher Note

Refer to the picture key for this week's sort. See Appendix B, "Sound Sort Picture Key."

Take the pictures from your own bag and spread them out on the table in front of you. Hold up the *cake* picture, and have the students say its name. Hold up the *lake* picture and have the students say its name. Then ask:

Q Do cake *and* lake *rhyme?*

Confirm that the words *cake* and *lake* do rhyme. Model placing the cards on the table side by side, away from the unsorted cards. Explain that you are putting the pictures side by side because *cake* and *lake* rhyme.

Hold up the *duck* picture, and have the students say its name. Then ask:

Q *Which picture rhymes with* duck?

Confirm that *truck* rhymes with *duck*. Hold up the *truck* picture and place it next to the *duck* picture on the table in front of you to form a rhyming pair.

Distribute one bag of sorting pictures to each student. Remind the students that they will sort these pictures into rhyming pairs during independent word work. Review that they will not use a sorting guide this week. Explain that they will find the two pictures whose names rhyme and put them on the table side by side. Tell them that when they are finished sorting, they will say the name of each pair to make sure they rhyme. Ask and briefly discuss:

Q *How will you find pictures whose names rhyme?*

> **Students might say:**
>
> "I can take the first picture and then say the names of the other pictures until I find the rhyme."
>
> "I can say the names of the pictures until I find two that rhyme and then take that pair, like a memory game."

Tell the students that if they need help remembering how to sort their pictures during independent word work, they may quietly ask another student in their reading group to remind them. Have them put their sorting pictures in their bags and their bags in their toolboxes.

5 Introduce the High-frequency Word *Were*

were   "Some girls were jumping rope at recess yesterday."

Introduce *were* by saying the word as you show the word card to the students. Use the word in a sentence. Have the students read it and spell it twice, and then read it a third time.

6 Review High-frequency Words

Review the previously introduced high-frequency words by showing each word in the review deck and having the students read it, spell it, and read it again.

7 Read *The Spelling Test*

Distribute a copy of *The Spelling Test* to each student. Tell the students that they will read this book today. Read the title aloud and identify the names of the author and illustrator. Tell the students that this story is about children getting ready for a test at school. Open to page 1, and ask the students to find today's new word, *were*. Then turn to page 2, and ask the students to find the new words *could* and *should*. Finally, turn to page 9, and ask the students to find the new word *would*.

Write the words *o'clock*, *knew*, *word*, *eyes*, and *read* on your wipe-off board. Read them for the students one at a time and have the students say each word. Tell the students that they will see these words in today's story. Explain they will have to remember these words when they see them, or ask you for help. Leave the words on the wipe-off board as a reminder and place the board where everyone can see it. Then have the students turn to page 1 in their books and read the story in quiet voices.

Teacher Note

Add the word card for *were* to the high-frequency word card review deck.

Monitor the students as they read, and support any student who struggles. When all the students have finished reading, ask and briefly discuss:

Q *What is this story about?*

Q *How does Cliff learn to spell well?*

Have the students put their books in their toolboxes. Remind the students that when they go to independent reading, they will read today's book before reading the other books in their toolboxes.

GUIDED SPELLING

long	"The movie was so long that I fell asleep."
slam	"Don't let the door slam when you shut it."
very	"I'm in a very good mood today."

Guide the students through spelling each of the decodable words, paying particular attention to sounds that can be spelled in more than one way. Then have them write the high-frequency word.

In this lesson, the students:

- Produce rhymes
- Review spelling-sounds
- Review high-frequency words
- Read a familiar book

Materials

- Teacher and student copies of *The Spelling Test* from Day 2
- Sound card review deck
- High-frequency word card review deck
- Wipe-off board, dry-erase marker, and tissue or cloth
- Group set of the "Individual Reading Observation" sheet (IR1), from Week 5

1 Phonological Awareness: Producing Rhymes

Have the students add each of the following sounds to make words that rhyme with *an*, after you say the phonemes:

/j/	(Jan)
/m/	(man)
/d/	(Dan)
/v/	(van)
/r/	(ran)
/pl/	(plan)

2 Review Spelling-Sounds

Use the sound card review deck to have the students say the sound of each spelling.

3 Review High-frequency Words

Review the previously introduced high-frequency words by showing each word in the review deck and having the students read it, spell it, and read it again.

4 Reread *The Spelling Test*

Have the students take *The Spelling Test* from their toolboxes and tell them that they will reread this story today. Read the title aloud with the students. Write the words *o'clock, knew, word, eyes,* and *read* on your wipe-off board, say the words, and remind the students that they will see these words in today's book. Explain that they will have to remember these words when they see them, or ask for help. Leave the words on the wipe-off board as a reminder and place the board where everyone can see it.

Remind the students that if they finish reading, they will go back to the first page and read the book again. Have the students read *The Spelling Test* in quiet voices.

> ☑ **INDIVIDUAL READING OBSERVATION NOTE**
>
> Listen to a few students as they read, taking notes on the "Individual Reading Observation" sheet (IR1) and offering support as needed; see page 144 of the *Assessment Resource Book*.

5 Check Comprehension and Reflect

When all the students have finished reading, ask and briefly discuss:

Q *How does Cliff feel at the beginning of the story? How does Cliff feel at the end of the story? How do you know?*

Have the students return their books to their toolboxes. Remind them that when they go to independent reading, they will read today's book before reading the other books in their toolboxes.

GUIDED SPELLING

We can spell.

Guide the students through the sentence, word by word.

Spelling Support

spell: Remind the students that the sound /l/ at the end of a word is usually spelled *l-l*. Tell the students that in *spell* the sound /l/ is spelled *l-l*.

RESOURCES

New	Revisit	Practice or Reteach

Winter Fun	***The Spelling Test***	***The Clowns***
by Rob Arego, illustrated by Marjorie Leggitt	by Rob Arego, illustrated by Linda Pierce	by Rob Arego, illustrated by Asha Pearse

Reteaching
- "Reteach with *The Clowns*"

Assessment Resource Book
- Week 8 assessments

Sound Cards
- *sk* /sk/
- *sl* /sl/

High-frequency Word Cards
- *both*
- *does*

Wipe-off Boards

 ## Online Resources

Visit the CCC Learning Hub (ccclearninghub.org) to find your online resources for this week.

Assessment Forms
- "Mastery Test 6" record (MT6)
- "Mastery Test 6 Student Card" (SC6)

Reproducible
- "Set 3, Week 8 Sort" (BLM9)

OVERVIEW

Spelling-Sound Focus	High-frequency Words
• *sk* /sk/	• *both*
• *sl* /sl/	• *does*

⏱ DO AHEAD

✓ Prior to Day 1, add high-frequency word cards for *both* and *does* to the word wall if they are not already displayed.

✓ Prior to Day 2, visit the CCC Learning Hub (ccclearninghub.org) to access and print "Set 3, Week 8 Sort" (BLM9). Make a copy for each student in the group, plus one. Cut apart the pictures on each sheet (keeping one copy intact) to create a set of sorting pictures with rhyming pairs for each student in the group. Place each set of pictures in a resealable plastic bag.

✓ Prior to Day 3, add the sound cards for *sk* and *sl* to the sound card review deck.

✓ Prior to Day 3, make a copy of the "Mastery Test 6" record (MT6) for each student in the group; see page 173 of the *Assessment Resource Book*.

✓ Prior to Day 3, make one copy of the "Mastery Test 6 Student Card" (SC6); see page 174 of the *Assessment Resource Book*.

🌐 ELL SUPPORT

▪ **sl**

There are no initial or final *s* blends in Spanish. The spelling *sl* only occurs in separate syllables, such as in *isla* (EES-lah), "island." The students may add a vowel sound before the initial consonant in words with *s* blends.

▪ **sk**

The *s* blend /sk/ occurs in Spanish at syllable junctures. It can be spelled *sc* as in *escuela* (ehs-KWAY-lah), "school," or *squ* as in *bosque* (BOHS-kay), "forest."

(continues)

🌐 ELL SUPPORT *(continued)*

- **sk, sl**

  There are no initial or final consonant blends in Chinese. Students may insert a slight vowel sound between the consonants. When they encounter a final consonant blend, they may add a syllable or drop the last consonant.

- **does**

  Introduce *does* by explaining that you use it when you are talking with a friend about someone else. Contrast *does* with *do* to clarify the difference for the students: *I do. You do. Ana does.* Ask the students a series of questions, and prompt them to answer in both the positive and negative. For example, you might ask, "Does your brother like to [read/jump/paint]?" and have the students answer, "Yes, he does" or "No, he does not." Invite the students to ask each other questions that begin with *does*.

In this lesson, the students:

- Practice oral blending
- Learn the consonant blend *sk* /sk/
- Read decodable words
- Learn the high-frequency word *both*
- Review high-frequency words
- Read a familiar book

Materials

- Teacher and student copies of *The Spelling Test* from Week 7
- Wipe-off board, dry-erase marker, and tissue or cloth
- High-frequency word card for *both*
- High-frequency word card review deck

1 Phonological Awareness: Oral Blending

Have the students blend each of the words that follow after you say the phonemes, using continuous blending. Clap softly as you say each sound. Then brush your hands past each other as the students say the word.

/jēp/	jeep
/gāt/	gate
/ssāff/	safe
/hhōp/	hope
/bīk/	bike
/mmūll/	mule

2 Introduce the Consonant Blend *sk* /sk/

Explain that today the students will learn a pair of letters that they will often see together at the beginning of words. Write the spelling *sk* on your wipe-off board. Explain that when students see the letters *s* and *k* together, they will blend the sounds. Point to the left of *sk* and sweep under the spelling as you say /sk/. Have the students blend the sounds as you sweep under the spelling. Then say each of the words that follow, emphasizing the beginning blend. Have the students repeat each word: *skin, sky, skip.*

Tell the students that they will also see *s* and *k* together at the end of words. Say each of the words that follow, emphasizing the ending blend. Have the students repeat each word: *task, risk, mask.*

Have the students each trace the spelling *sk* on the table in front of them with one finger as they say /sk/.

Teacher Note

You may wish to explain that a *mule* is an animal that is like a donkey.

 ELL Note

You may wish to have the students practice saying additional words beginning with *sk*, such as **sk**irt, **sk**ate, and **sk**it.

Decoding Support

Support struggling students by covering the ending (including any doubled consonant) and having the students read the base word alone. Then uncover the ending and have them read the entire word. Another option is to write just the base word, have the students read that, double the final consonant if needed, add the ending, and have the students read the inflected word.

Teacher Note

Add the word card for *both* to the high-frequency word card review deck.

3 Read Decodable Words

Write the following words on your wipe-off board:

skill	ask
skidding	stuck
must	rushed

Point to each word and sweep under it as the students read it.

4 Introduce the High-frequency Word *Both*

both   "Both of my sisters are older than I am."

Introduce *both* by saying the word as you show the word card to the students. Use the word in a sentence. Have the students read it and spell it twice, and then read it a third time.

5 Review High-frequency Words

Review the previously introduced high-frequency words by showing each word in the review deck and having the students read it, spell it, and read it again.

6 Reread *The Spelling Test*

Have the students take the book *The Spelling Test* from their toolboxes. Tell the students that they will reread this book today. Read the title with the students and ask:

Q *What happens in this story?*

Have a few volunteers share their thinking with the group. Then have the students read the book in quiet voices.

Monitor the students as they read, and support any student who struggles. When all the students have finished reading, collect the books or have the students return their books to their toolboxes.

GUIDED SPELLING

skid	"Cars can skid on icy roads."
fast	"How fast can you run?"
could	"If fish had legs, do you think they could walk?"

Guide the students through spelling each of the decodable words, paying particular attention to sounds that can be spelled in more than one way. Then have them write the high-frequency word.

In this lesson, the students:

- Practice oral segmenting
- Learn the consonant blend *sl* /sl/
- Read decodable words
- Learn the high-frequency word *does*
- Review high-frequency words
- Read a new book

1 Phonological Awareness: Oral Segmenting

Have the students segment the phonemes after you say each of the words that follow. Have them clap softly as they say each sound.

note	/n/ /ō/ /t/
tune	/t/ /o͞o/ /n/
game	/g/ /ā/ /m/
Mike	/m/ /ī/ /k/
read	/r/ /ē/ /d/
whale	/hw/ /ā/ /l/

2 Introduce the Consonant Blend *sl* /sl/

Explain that today the students will learn a pair of letters that they will often see together at the beginning of words. Write the spelling *sl* on your wipe-off board. Explain that when the students see the letters *s* and *l* together, they will blend the sounds. Point to the left of *sl* and sweep under the spelling as you say /sl/. Have the students blend the sounds as you sweep under the spelling. Then say each of the words that follow, emphasizing the beginning blend. Have the students repeat each word: *slime, slip, slow.*

Have the students each trace the spelling *sl* on the table in front of them with one finger as they say /sl/.

Materials

- Teacher and student copies of *Winter Fun*
- Wipe-off board, dry-erase marker, and tissue or cloth
- Student bags of sorting pictures, prepared ahead from "Set 3, Week 8 Sort" (BLM9)
- Intact copy of "Set 3, Week 8 Sort" (BLM9), prepared ahead
- High-frequency word card for *does*
- High-frequency word card review deck

ELL Note

You may wish to have the students practice saying additional words beginning with /sl/, such as **sl**eep, **sl**ope, and **sl**am.

Teacher Note

You may wish to explain that *slick* means "slippery."

Teacher Note

Refer to the picture key for this week's sort. See Appendix B, "Sound Sort Picture Key."

Teacher Note

Add the word card for *does* to the high-frequency word card review deck.

3 Read Decodable Words

Write the following words on your wipe-off board:

slick	grip
sled	clapping
slid	fast

Point to each word and sweep under it as the students read it.

4 Introduce the Sound Sort

Display the intact "Set 3, Week 8 Sort" sheet (BLM9) and explain that these are the pictures the students will sort this week. Just as they did last week, they will make pairs of pictures whose names rhyme. Point to each picture and say its name. Then have the students say the names as you point to the pictures.

Distribute one bag of sorting pictures to each student. Remind them that they will find two pictures whose names rhyme and put them next to each other. Tell them that when they are finished sorting, they will check their sorts by saying the name of each picture in a pair to make sure they rhyme.

Have the students put their bags in their toolboxes.

5 Introduce the High-frequency Word *Does*

does   "What sound does a cow make?"

Introduce *does* by saying the word as you show the word card to the students. Use the word in a sentence. Have the students read it and spell it twice, and then read it a third time.

6 Review High-frequency Words

Review the previously introduced high-frequency words by showing each word in the review deck and having the students read it, spell it, and read it again.

7 Read *Winter Fun*

Distribute a copy of *Winter Fun* to each student. Tell the students that they will read this book today. Read the title aloud to the students and identify the names of the author and illustrator. Tell the students that this book is about winter sports. Open to page 2, and ask the students to find today's new word, *does*. Then point to page 3, and ask the students to find the new word *both*.

Write the word *skill* on your wipe-off board and have the students read the word. Explain that a *skill* is something that you practice to learn to do, like dribbling a basketball or riding a bike. You don't do these things the first time you try, you have to practice to get good at them. Write the words *winter*, *ice*, *take*, and *snow* on your wipe-off board. Read them for the students one at a time and have the students say each word. Tell the students that they will see these words in today's book. Explain that they will have to remember these words when they see them, or ask you for help. Leave the words on the wipe-off board as a reminder and place the board where everyone can see it. Then have the students turn to page 1 in their books and read the story in quiet voices.

Monitor the students as they read, and support any student who struggles. When all the students have finished reading, ask and briefly discuss:

Q *What are some of the things that people can do in winter?*

Q *Why does ice skating take a lot of skill?*

Have the students put their books in their toolboxes. Remind the students that when they go to independent reading, they will read today's book before reading the other books in their toolboxes.

GUIDED SPELLING

sled	"It's fun to ride a sled down a hill."
slick	"Ice will make the sidewalk slick."
were	"Where were you born?"

Guide the students through spelling each of the decodable words, paying particular attention to sounds that can be spelled in more than one way. Then have them write the high-frequency word.

Spelling Support

slick: Remind the students that the sound /k/ at the end of a word is usually spelled *c-k*. Tell the students that in *slick* the sound /k/ is spelled *c-k*.

Winter Fun
Produce Rhymes;
Review and Reread

Materials

- Teacher and student copies of *Winter Fun* from Day 2
- Sound card review deck
- High-frequency word card review deck
- Wipe-off board, dry-erase marker, and tissue or cloth
- "Mastery Test 6" record (MT6) for each student
- One copy of "Mastery Test 6 Student Card" (SC6)

In this lesson, the students:

- Produce rhyming words
- Review spelling-sounds
- Review high-frequency words
- Read a familiar book

1 Phonological Awareness: Producing Rhymes

Have the students add each of the following sounds to make words that rhyme with *it*, after you say the phonemes:

/b/	(bit)
/f/	(fit)
/k/	(kit)
/l/	(lit)
/s/	(sit)
/p/	(pit)
/m/	(mitt)

2 Review Spelling-Sounds

Use the sound card review deck to have the students say the sound of each spelling.

3 Review High-frequency Words

Review the previously introduced high-frequency words by showing each word in the review deck and having the students read it, spell it, and read it again.

4 Reread *Winter Fun*

Have the students take *Winter Fun* from their toolboxes. Tell the students that they will reread this book today. Read the title aloud with the students. Write the words *winter, ice, take,* and *snow* on your wipe-off board, say the words, and remind the students that they will see these words in today's story. Explain that they will have to remember these words when they see them, or ask you for help. Leave the words on the wipe-off board as a reminder and place the board where everyone can see it.

Remind the students that if they finish reading early, they will go back to the first page and read the book again. Have the students read *Winter Fun* in quiet voices.

5 Check Comprehension and Reflect

When all the students have finished reading, ask and briefly discuss:

Q *What did you learn from in this book?*

Q *Which sports look fun to you? Why?*

Have the students return their books to their toolboxes. Remind them that when they go to independent reading, they will read today's book before reading the other books in their toolboxes.

 MASTERY TEST ASSESSMENT NOTE

Administer Mastery Test 6 after this lesson, using "Mastery Test 6" (MT6) and "Mastery Test 6 Student Card" (SC6); see pages 173–174 of the *Assessment Resource Book*.

If you identify students who need to repeat instruction, first determine which sounds and high-frequency words the student missed. Then use "Reteach with *The Band*" on page 78 and "Reteach with *The Clowns*" below to reteach needed content. Administer Mastery Test 6 again after reteaching.

GUIDED SPELLING

> We could slip.

Guide the students through the sentence, word by word.

RETEACHING

Reteach with *The Clowns*

Review the spelling-sounds *sp* /sp/, *cl* /kl/, *sk* /sk/, and *sl* /sl/, and the high-frequency words *could, would, should, were, both,* and *does*. Use *The Clowns* for reading practice.

After reading the title aloud to the students, write the words *clown, circus,* and *climbs* on your wipe-off board, say the words, and have the students say them. Explain that the students will see these words in today's book. Tell the students that they will have to remember these words when they see them, or ask you for help. Leave the words on your

Teacher Note

You may wish to have students who do not require reteaching put *The Clowns* in their toolboxes for independent reading. If so, introduce the words *clown, circus,* and *climbs* by writing them on your wipe-off board, saying the words, and explaining that the students will see these words in the book.

Teacher Note

Mastery Test 6 follows this lesson. You may wish to omit Guided Spelling today and use the time to administer mastery tests. Have the students read books from previous weeks during this time.

Teacher Note

If you have students who are struggling to learn the sounds and words you have taught in the previous two weeks, you might provide an additional week of instruction before introducing new sounds and words. For more information, see "Reteaching" in the Introduction.

Teacher Note

Administer Mastery Test 6 again after reteaching. See "Mastery Test Assessment Note" on the previous page.

wipe-off board as a reminder and place the board where everyone can see it.

Explain that the students will read the book in quiet voices. Review that students who finish reading early will go back to the first page and read the book again. Have the students read *The Clowns*.

When all the students have finished reading, ask and briefly discuss:

Q *What are some things the clowns in the circus do?*

Q *Have you ever seen a clown? Tell us about it.*

Collect the books or have the students put their books in their toolboxes.

Appendices

HIGH-FREQUENCY WORD INDEX

High-frequency Word	Where Taught
a	Shared Reading, Grade K, Week 4
after	Set 5, Week 1
again	Set 3, Week 4
and	Shared Reading, Grade K, Week 3
answer	Set 5, Week 12
are	Shared Reading, Grade K, Week 5
be	Set 3, Week 1
because	Set 5, Week 5
been	Set 5, Week 10
both	Set 3, Week 8
boy	Set 4, Week 2
brother	Set 4, Week 1
by	Set 1, Week 7
can	Shared Reading, Grade K, Week 6
can't	Set 1, Week 2
change	Set 5, Week 14
children	Set 5, Week 5
cold	Set 4, Week 4
come	Set 2, Week 7
could	Set 3, Week 7
do	Set 2, Week 3
does	Set 3, Week 8
don't	Set 4, Week 6
down	Set 1, Week 5
earth	Set 5, Week 14
enough	Set 5, Week 10
even	Set 5, Week 7

High-frequency Word	Where Taught
ever	Set 5, Week 3
every	Set 4, Week 1
father	Set 4, Week 8
few	Set 5, Week 11
find	Set 5, Week 11
for	Set 3, Week 4
four	Set 5, Week 12
from	Set 3, Week 3
get	Set 1, Week 3
give	Set 5, Week 4
go	Set 1, Week 5
good	Set 3, Week 2
great	Set 5, Week 8
have	Set 2, Week 4
he	Set 1, Week 1
head	Set 5, Week 2
her	Set 2, Week 6
here	Set 1, Week 7
his	Set 2, Week 6
home	Set 2, Week 4
I	Shared Reading, Grade K, Week 4
is	Shared Reading, Grade K, Week 8
isn't	Set 1, Week 2
kind	Set 5, Week 11
large	Set 5, Week 13
learn	Set 5, Week 13
like	Set 2, Week 3
little	Set 2, Week 1

(continues)

High-frequency Word	Where Taught
live	Set 5, Week 4
look	Set 3, Week 2
make	Set 3, Week 1
many	Set 3, Week 5
me	Shared Reading, Grade K, Week 4
mind	Set 5, Week 11
most	Set 5, Week 14
mother	Set 4, Week 1
move	Set 5, Week 8
my	Set 1, Week 6
never	Set 5, Week 3
no	Set 1, Week 4
of	Set 2, Week 5
old	Set 4, Week 4
once	Set 5, Week 9
one	Set 4, Week 5
only	Set 5, Week 3
other	Set 4, Week 1
out	Set 2, Week 7
over	Set 4, Week 3
people	Set 3, Week 5
picture	Set 5, Week 7
put	Set 2, Week 2
read	Set 5, Week 2
said	Set 2, Week 5
saw	Set 1, Week 8
say	Set 2, Week 8
says	Set 2, Week 8
school	Set 4, Week 7
see	Shared Reading, Grade K, Week 4
she	Set 1, Week 1
should	Set 3, Week 7
so	Set 2, Week 8
some	Set 2, Week 7

High-frequency Word	Where Taught
talk	Set 5, Week 5
the	Shared Reading, Grade K, Week 3
their	Set 4, Week 4
there	Set 3, Week 1
they	Set 1, Week 8
though	Set 5, Week 9
thought	Set 4, Week 8
to	Set 1, Week 3
told	Set 4, Week 4
too	Set 4, Week 6
toward	Set 4, Week 3
two	Set 4, Week 5
very	Set 3, Week 6
walk	Set 5, Week 5
want	Set 3, Week 3
was	Set 2, Week 1
watch	Set 5, Week 10
water	Set 3, Week 3
we	Shared Reading, Grade K, Week 5
were	Set 3, Week 7
what	Set 2, Week 2
where	Set 1, Week 6
who	Set 4, Week 7
woman	Set 4, Week 2
women	Set 4, Week 2
won't	Set 4, Week 6
word	Set 5, Week 12
work	Set 5, Week 1
would	Set 3, Week 7
yes	Set 1, Week 4
you	Shared Reading, Grade K, Week 4
young	Set 5, Week 13
your	Set 3, Week 6

SOUND SORT PICTURE KEY

Set 3, Week 1 Sort

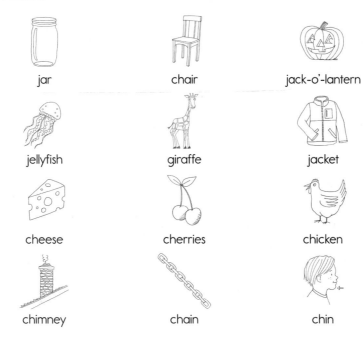

jar	chair	jack-o'-lantern
jellyfish	giraffe	jacket
cheese	cherries	chicken
chimney	chain	chin

Set 3, Week 2 Sort

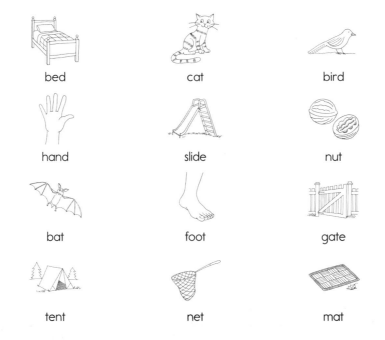

bed	cat	bird
hand	slide	nut
bat	foot	gate
tent	net	mat

Set 3, Week 3 Sort

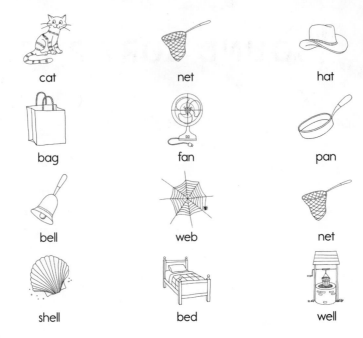

cat	net	hat
bag	fan	pan
bell	web	net
shell	bed	well

Set 3, Week 4 Sort

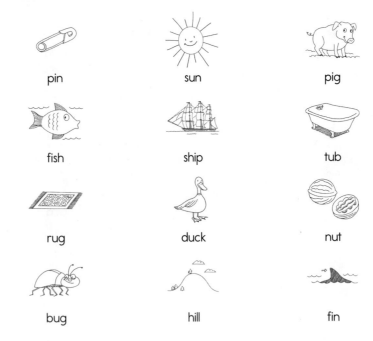

pin	sun	pig
fish	ship	tub
rug	duck	nut
bug	hill	fin

Set 3, Week 5 Sort

fan	cat	van
pan	bat	hat
can	man	mat
rat		

Set 3, Week 6 Sort

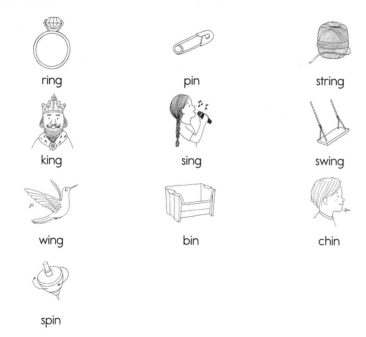

ring	pin	string
king	sing	swing
wing	bin	chin
spin		

Set 3, Week 7 Sort

cake	lake	chain
train	clock	block
duck	truck	chair
bear	ring	swing

Set 3, Week 8 Sort

sock	lock	ball
wall	pool	stool
flag	bag	log
frog	moon	spoon